Science 3

for Christian Schools®

BJU PRESS
GREENVILLE, SOUTH CAROLINA

Science 3

for Christian Schools®

Second Edition

Dawn L. Watkins

Consultants
  Joseph Henson, Ph.D. Chairman, Division of Natural Science, Bob Jones University
  Brian S. Vogt, Ph.D. Professor, Department of Chemistry, Bob Jones University

Special acknowledgment is given to Candace J. Levesque for organizing the scope and sequence of the project.

SCIENCE 3 for Christian Schools®
Second Edition

Dawn L. Watkins

Design	Composition	Project Manager
Elly Kalagayan	Kelley Moore	Vic Ludlum
Wendy Searles		
John Bjerk		

Produced in cooperation with the Bob Jones University Department of Science Education of the School of Education, the College of Arts and Science, and Bob Jones Elementary School.

Photo credits appear on pages 198-99.

for Christian Schools is a registered trademark of BJU Press.

ISBN 1-59166-427-6

15 14 13 12 11 10 9 8 7 6 5 4 3 2

Contents

1

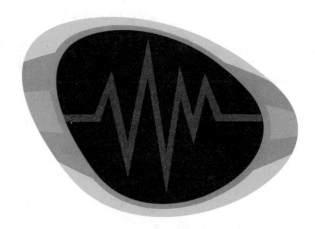

Sound

God created our world in six days. Men have gazed at it in wonder for thousands of years. Sometimes men write down what they see, or *observe*. They try to describe what God has made.

Scientists try to record what they learn about our world. They try to measure things, to tell how things look, to give things names. You can be a scientist if you observe and record what you see or hear. You can learn to measure, to describe, and to find out.

You can find out about sound. Can you remember some of the sounds you have heard so far today? What was the loudest sound? What was the softest? Can you tell anything else about the sounds?

"And Zadok the priest took an horn of oil out of the tabernacle, and anointed Solomon. And they blew the trumpet; and all the people said, God save king Solomon. And all the people came up after him, and the people piped with pipes, and rejoiced with great joy, so that the earth rent with the sound of them."

I Kings 1:39-40

2

What Causes Sound?

Put two fingers on your throat and hum. What do you feel? When you hum, you cause a *vibration*. A vibration is a moving back and forth. A hum causes parts of your throat to move back and forth.

Read the next sentence aloud with your fingers on your throat. Can you still feel vibrations? What does that tell you about how people speak?

Listen for a moment without speaking or humming. What sounds do you hear right now? What is making those sounds?

Can you touch anything that is making a sound? Is it vibrating or moving? Do you find that where there is sound there is always movement?

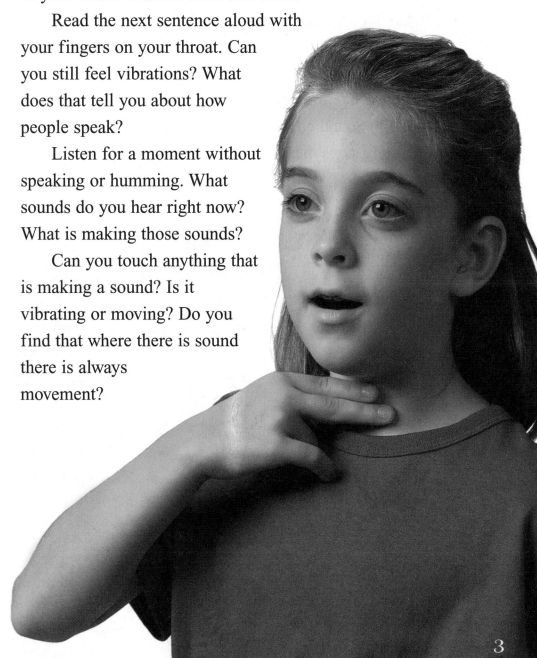

How Does Sound Travel?

Have you ever thrown a stone into a pond or a puddle? What happened to the water when you dropped the stone in? The water moved out from the spot in rings of waves. The rings rippled out until they struck dry land. After a while the water stopped making waves and was still again.

Sound can make ripples in the air. The ripples are something like the ripples on the water, but you cannot see them. Sound goes out in waves through the air until something stops them or bounces them back.

Sound waves go out from their source in all directions. How does that make them different from the water waves?

When sound waves hit an object, they are either *absorbed*—taken in—or they are *reflected*—bounced back. If a sound bounces back well enough for us to hear it again, it is an *echo*.

Large, hard surfaces reflect sound better than other surfaces. Canyons often produce many echoes when sound bounces off their rock walls. But more than a sound and a good surface are needed to make an echo.

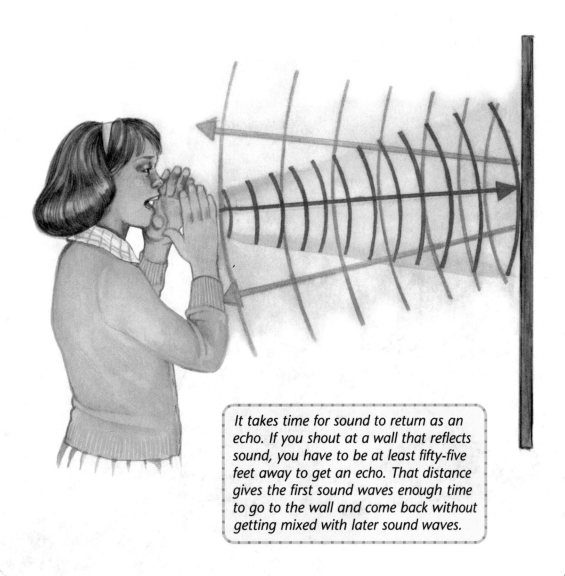

It takes time for sound to return as an echo. If you shout at a wall that reflects sound, you have to be at least fifty-five feet away to get an echo. That distance gives the first sound waves enough time to go to the wall and come back without getting mixed with later sound waves.

What kinds of surfaces do you think absorb sound? Big rooms sometimes echo sound. Special ceilings can take in some of the sound waves. Carpeting and drapes can also soak up some of the sound waves. Why do you think many ceiling tiles have rough surfaces?

What are the men adding to this room that will absorb sound?

Can you name some things that vibrate to make sound? Does a violin string vibrate? Does a kazoo? Does a drum? What kind of movement causes vibrations? Vibrations can be made by plucking, rubbing, blowing, and hitting. How are sounds being made in this picture?

Any object that vibrates makes the air around it vibrate. Do you think that sound waves can make other materials vibrate?

7

Finding Out...

About Sound

1. Get

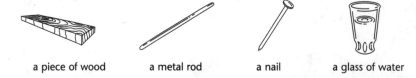

a piece of wood   a metal rod   a nail   a glass of water

2. Work with a partner. Put your ear against one end of the piece of wood. Have your partner tap the other end with the nail. Now raise your head and have your partner tap the wood again. Which tap could you hear better?

3. Try the same experiment with the metal rod and the glass of water.

4. Have your partner try all three tests.

5. Record your findings.

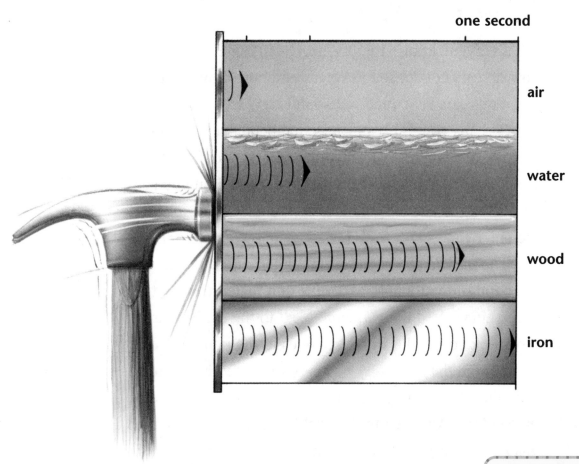

one second

air

water

wood

iron

A long time ago men sometimes put an ear to the train tracks to find out how far away the train was. Why would that work?

Sound waves can travel through solids, liquids, and gases. Air is made of gases. We hear many sounds that travel through air. What are some sounds that you hear right now that are coming to you through the air?

Sound travels faster through water than it does through air. It travels faster through wood than it does through water. It travels faster through most metals than it does through wood.

How Do We Hear Sound?

Everyone knows that we hear with our ears. But just how do ears collect sound waves and how do we know when our ears have received sound waves?

Perhaps you think an ear is that bendable thing on the side of your head. That is one part of your ear. It is the *outer ear*. Look at someone's outer ear. Can you see an opening to a small tunnel? That tunnel is also part of the outer ear.

The *middle ear* begins at the other end of the tunnel. That end of the tunnel has a very thin material over it—a membrane called the *eardrum*. Next to the eardrum are three tiny bones, the smallest bones in the body.

Behind the three tiny bones is an oval window that goes into the *inner ear*. In there is a coiled part called the *cochlea*. Attached to the cochlea is a *nerve* that goes to the brain.

Where do you think sound waves go after they are "captured" by the outer ear? They travel down the tunnel to the eardrum. The eardrum vibrates when the sound waves hit it. What do you think vibrates then?

sounds

> *Why should you never stick anything into your ear?*

The vibrations from the small bones go around the coil of the cochlea. When they reach a certain nerve, the nerve sends a message to the brain. Why do messages go there?

What would happen if the eardrum or the small bones of the middle ear were damaged?

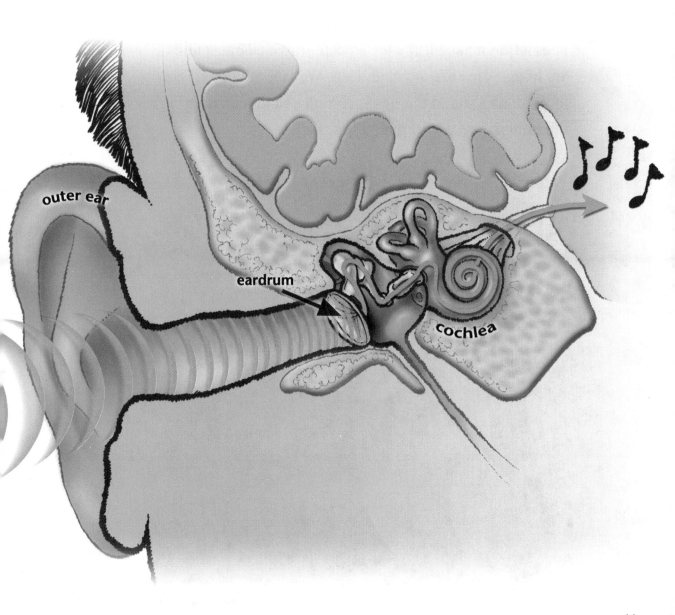

outer ear

eardrum

cochlea

How Do We Judge Sound?

Can you think of something that makes a loud sound? Can you think of a soft sound? What do you think makes the difference between the two sounds? A loud sound has stronger vibrations than a soft one.

What kind of sound would you say a mouse makes? Do you think it is a high, squeaky sound? What sound does a lion make? It makes a deep growl. Some sounds are high. Some are low and deep. We call the highness or lowness of a sound the *pitch*. A high sound has more vibrations in a second than a low sound.

Name a sound you like to hear. What do you like about it? Do you like the sound itself? Or do you like the sound because it means something special or someone special is nearby?

Can you think of a sound that you do not like to hear? What makes you not like it? Some sounds are too loud or too high for the ear. Some sounds are displeasing to the ear. When we talk about how much we like or do not like a sound, we are talking about sound *quality*.

Too much of a loud, harsh sound can hurt the eardrum. Sometimes the eardrum never heals.

Rock music, jackhammers, and big machines are bad for the eardrum. People who are around such sounds for a long time often lose some of their hearing.

Do you like the sound of a power saw? Is it a pleasing sound? Some people think ocean waves make a pleasing sound. Most people enjoy the pleasing sounds of good music.

14

About Loudness and Pitch

1. Get

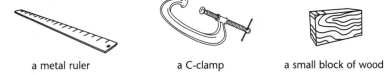

a metal ruler   a C-clamp   a small block of wood

2. Clamp the block of wood with the ruler under it to the edge of a desk. Let ten inches of the ruler hang off the edge. Let the ruler touch the clamp. Make the clamp tight.

3. Push the ruler down gently with your finger. Slide your finger off the ruler. Watch what happens. Listen to what happens.

4. Move the ruler back under the clamp another two inches. Repeat the test. Does the sound it makes have a higher or lower pitch?

5. Record your findings.

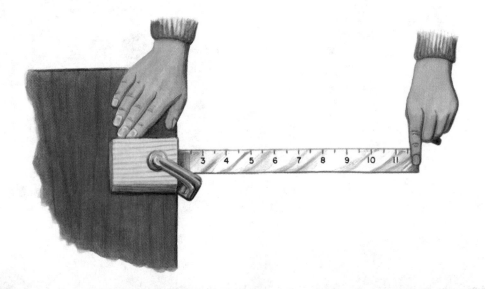

"So the people shouted when the priests blew with the trumpets: and it came to pass, when the people heard the sound of the trumpet, and the people shouted with a great shout, that the wall fell down flat, so that the people went up into the city, every man straight before him, and they took the city."   Joshua 6:20

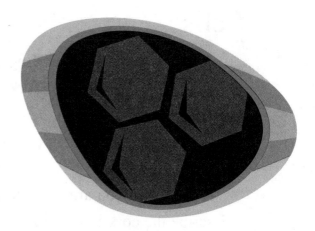

Cells, Tissues, and Organs

CHAPTER TWO

Cells

About 300 years ago an English scientist, Robert Hooke, looked at a piece of cork under his microscope. Then he wrote down what the cork looked like close up. Here is a photograph of cork as it may have looked to him.

Pretend that you are Robert Hooke. How would you describe the cork in a report?

Robert Hooke wrote about "little boxes" in his report. Did you include that in your description? What do the rows look like to you? Robert Hooke thought that they looked like rooms or chambers. Our word *cell* comes from a Latin word meaning "chamber." How is a cell like a chamber?

Many scientists began using microscopes to help them find out things. Much later, scientists learned that all living things are made of these tiny boxes called cells. For example, did you know your blood, muscles, and skin are made of cells? Leaves and flowers are made of cells too.

Why are the spaces in a bee's honeycomb called cells?

19

Finding Out... About Cells

1. Get

a microscope

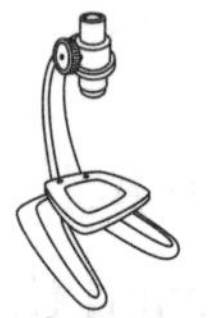

a green leaf

a microscope slide

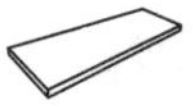

2. Peel off the bottom layer of the leaf and put it on a microscope slide.

3. Look at the leaf bottom under the microscope.

4. Record what you see.

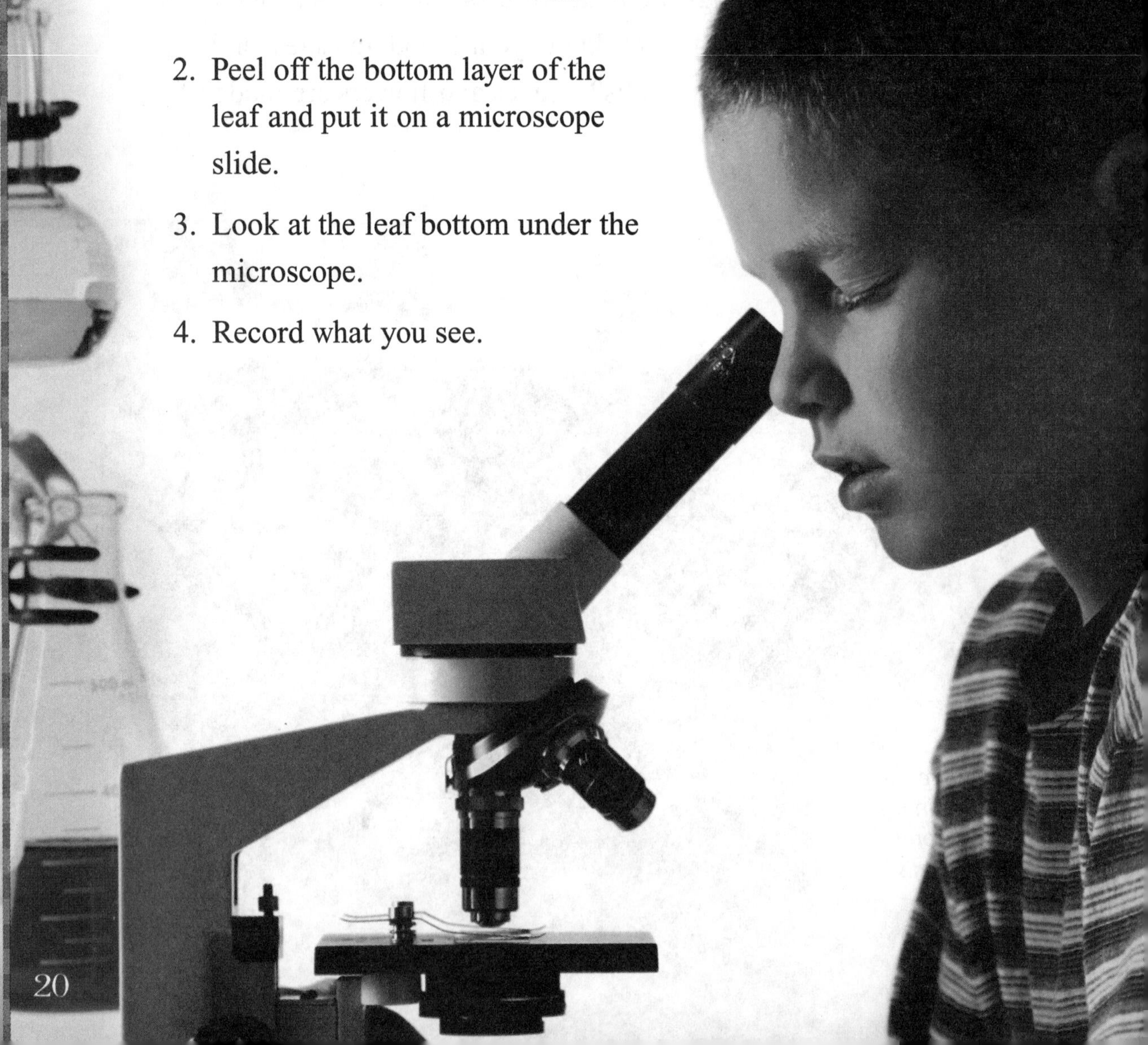

The yolk of an ostrich egg is the size of a softball.

A cell is the smallest living part of any living thing. Not all cells are the same size. Some can be seen only under a microscope. Some cells are so small that if 50,000 of them lined up, the row would be only one inch long.

Some cells are rather large. The yolk of an egg is one cell.

Big or small, all cells have the same main parts.
How many different parts do you see in this cell?

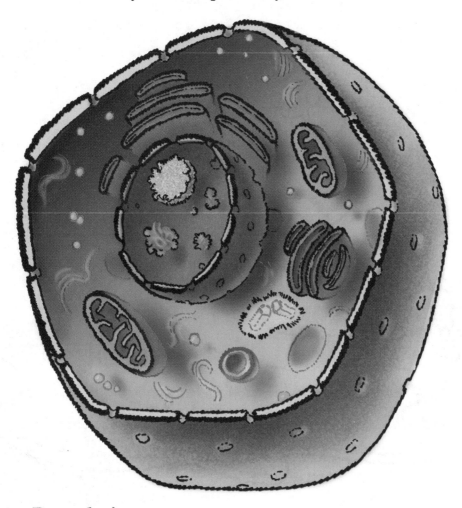

Boundaries

All cells have some kind of boundary. The outsides
of both plant and animal cells have soft, thin coverings
called *membranes*. A plant cell also has a *cell wall*
around the membrane. Plants have no bones. The
unbending cell walls give the plant support. Large trees
hold up branches weighing many tons.

The wood of one redwood could support the weight of a thousand elephants!

The largest trees alive today, the redwoods, exceed the weight of the largest land animals, the elephants, by more than one hundred times!

Wood is nothing more than plant cell walls. Did you know that paper is made from cell walls?

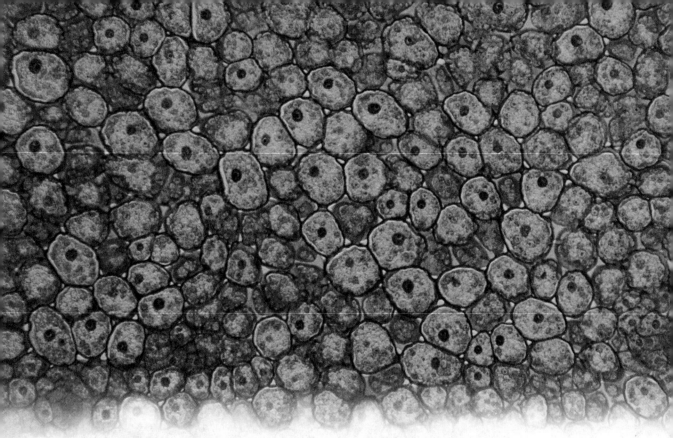

Animal cells do not have cell walls. Why do you think this is so? The boundary of animal cells is a *cell membrane*.

Nucleus

Do you see a large, dark part inside the cell? This is the *nucleus*. Nucleus comes from a word meaning "nut." Does it look like a nut to you? The nucleus is like a control center. It regulates the activities of the cell.

Cytoplasm

Cyto- means "cell," and *-plasm* means "fluid." What do you think cytoplasm is like? Cytoplasm surrounds the nucleus and is held in by the cell membrane. It is a fluid, something like thin jelly.

Tissues

Some cells, like egg yolks, function alone. Other cells work together in groups. A group of cells all doing the same kind of work makes a *tissue*. Some animal tissues are *blood, muscle,* and *bone.*

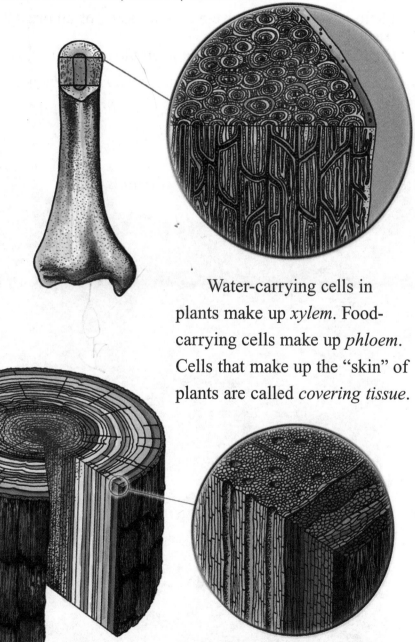

Water-carrying cells in plants make up *xylem*. Food-carrying cells make up *phloem*. Cells that make up the "skin" of plants are called *covering tissue*.

Organs

A group of tissues working together is an *organ*. Do you think a *heart* is an organ? What about a *brain?* Can you think of an organ that helps digest food?

An eye has muscles, fluid, nerves, and other parts that help in seeing. Is an eye a cell, a tissue, or an organ?

"For the invisible things of him from the creation of the world are clearly seen, being understood by the things that are made, even his eternal power and Godhead."

Romans 1:20

What animal do you think has the largest eye?

Putting Animals into Groups

"And out of the ground the Lord God formed every beast of the field, and every fowl of the air; and brought them unto Adam to see what he would call them: and whatsoever Adam called every living creature, that was the name thereof." *Genesis 2:19*

Do you know how many different kinds of animals there are? One hundred? Eight hundred? Seven thousand? There are many more than that. There are more than a million!

Imagine Adam naming all these animals.

wasp

batfish

How long do you think it would take to study the kinds one by one? Is there a better way to study them?

To study animals, scientists group or *classify* them. To classify means to find out how an animal is like or different from other animals. Scientists group together animals that are alike in certain ways.

jellyfish

chameleon

giraffe

29

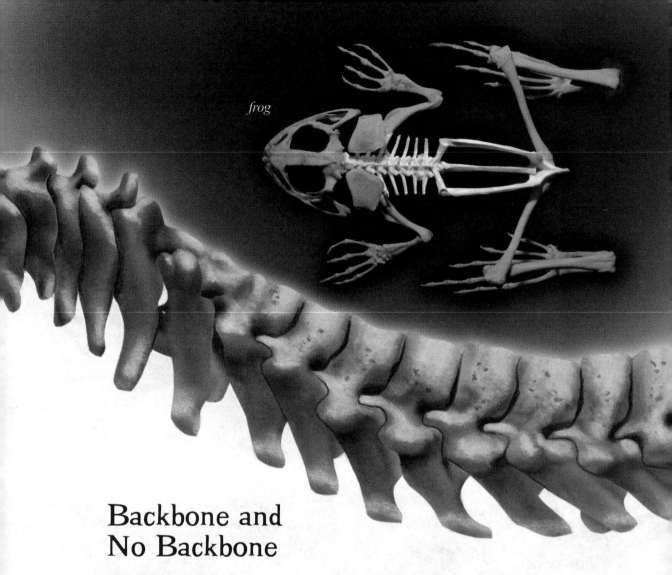

frog

Backbone and No Backbone

What is this? What is it made of? Why did the animal need it? What do you call the bones that go down the middle of the back?

Scientists group animals by how they are made. Some animals have backbones. Animals with backbones are called *vertebrates*.

Vertebrate comes from a word that means "to turn." What do you think a backbone helps an animal do?

How can you tell whether an animal has a backbone? Name some animals with backbones.

Animals with backbones usually have *limbs*—parts such as legs and wings. How many limbs do vertebrates usually have? Can you think of a vertebrate without limbs?

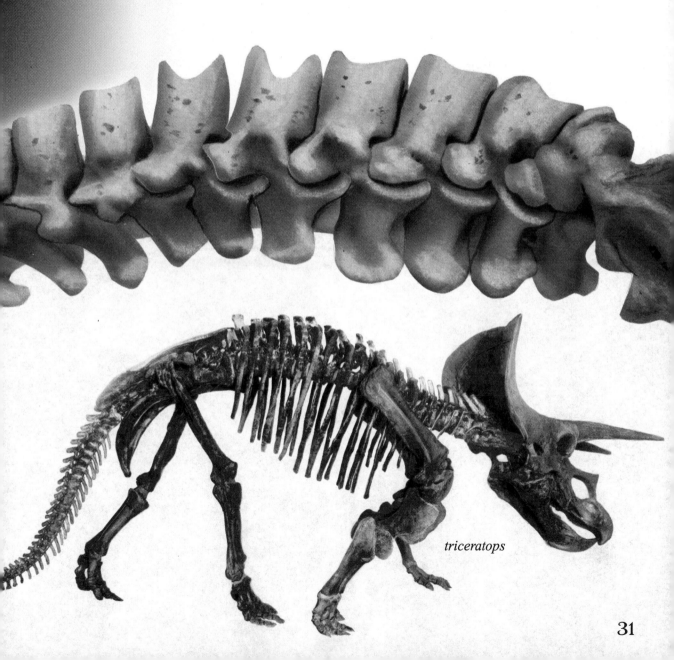

triceratops

This is a luna moth. It has two pairs of wings and six legs. Do you think this animal has a backbone?

There are many more animals without backbones than with backbones. You can discover the name for animals without backbones. Which word part would you put with *vertebrate* to name animals like the luna moth?

1. *sub-* which means "under"
2. *in-* which means "not"
3. *ex-* which means "out"

Warm-Blooded and Cold-Blooded

Animals with backbones can be put into smaller groups. They are either warm-blooded or cold-blooded.

How does the bird look? What is it trying to do? What is the dog doing? Why is it doing that? How does that help it?

The bird and the dog are both *warm-blooded*. Their body temperatures stay the same in cold or hot weather. Some animals can do things to help keep their temperatures the same. The bird fluffs its feathers to keep its temperature from dropping. The dog pants to keep its temperature from going up. How do other animals keep warm or cool?

snowy owl

Can you name some warm-blooded animals? How do you know they are warm-blooded?

hippopotamus

34

These are *cold-blooded* animals. That name does not mean that the blood of such animals is "cold." It means that the temperature of their blood does not stay the same all the time. What can you guess about the body temperatures of such animals?

The temperature of a cold-blooded animal goes up and down. If a crocodile is swimming in cold water, its temperature is lower than if it were in warm water. Would a snake in the shade or a snake in the sun have a higher body temperature?

grouper

toad

mangrove snake

35

Plant-Eating and Animal-Eating

Do lions eat hay? Do horses eat hamburgers? Do all animals eat the same things? Scientists sometimes group animals by what the animals eat.

Some animals eat only plants. Some animals eat only other animals. And some animals eat both plants and other animals. Can you think of an animal that eats only plants? A buffalo eats only plants. What does a zebra eat?

A lion eats only other animals. A bear eats other animals *and* some plants. Do you know of any other animals that eat both?

The word part -*vorous* means "eat." Here are three other word parts. Can you put each with *vorous* to name groups of animals by what they eat?

1. *carni*- which means "flesh"
2. *herbi*- which means "plant"
3. *omni*- which means "all"

What is the name for animals that eat both plants and animals?
What is the name for animals that eat plants?
What is the name for animals that eat other animals?

Finding Out...

About Cold-Blooded Animals

1. Get

ten or twelve live
ants or some
other insect

two jars with
lids

a dishpan

two trays of
ice cubes

2. Put half the ants in one jar and half the ants in the other jar. Watch the ants for a few minutes. Are they acting the same way in each jar?

3. Put the ice cubes in the dishpan. Put one jar of ants in the dishpan. Leave it in for at least ten minutes.

4. Take the jar out of the ice. Now look at the ants in both jars again.

5. Record any differences in how the ants in both jars move. Take the jars outside and let the ants go free.

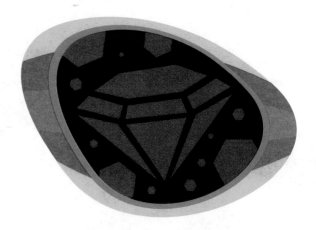

Minerals, Rocks, Soil

4

*"Surely there is a
vein for the silver, and a place
for gold where they fine it. Iron is taken out
of the earth, and brass is molten out of the stone. As
for the earth, out of it cometh bread: and under it is
turned up as it were fire. The stones of it are the place of
sapphires: and it hath dust of gold."*   *Job 28:1-2, 5-6*

Does the title of this chapter seem a little dull to
you? Do you think the earth is made just of dirt? God
has put good and shining treasures inside the earth.
Diamonds, emeralds, coal, gold, and platinum are just a
few of these riches. Can you name some more?

Minerals

Minerals are the small parts that make up rocks and mountains and the whole great ball we call our earth.

All mineral crystals have smooth, flat sides that meet in sharp edges and corners. Crystals come in all sizes and shapes. Some look like little clear boxes. Some have six sides. Others are shaped like pencils sticking up from a pencil holder. Some have unusual shapes, like the ones in the picture.

Every mineral has a crystal shape all its own. Salt crystals are different from all other crystals, and they always look the same. Diamond crystals always look alike and are different from all other kinds of crystals. Scientists use the shapes of crystals to tell minerals apart.

Scientists sometimes use color to tell one mineral from another. Minerals come in almost any color you can think of—like green, blue, black, red, gray, yellow, and pink. Can you think of a lavender mineral?

The hardness of a mineral also helps scientists tell what kind it is. *Talc* is a very soft mineral. Do you know what the hardest mineral is? A diamond is the hardest.

Finding Out...

About Mineral Crystals

1. Get

a pan

one-half cup of
water

a tablespoon
of salt

two shallow
dishes

2. Boil the water and dissolve the salt in it.

3. Pour half the salt water into one dish and half into
   the other.

4. Set one dish in a warm place. Set the other in a cool
   place. Leave them for several days.

5. When you check the dishes again, see if one dish
   has bigger crystals in it. What can you record about
   how temperature makes crystals form?

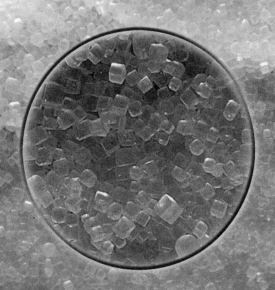

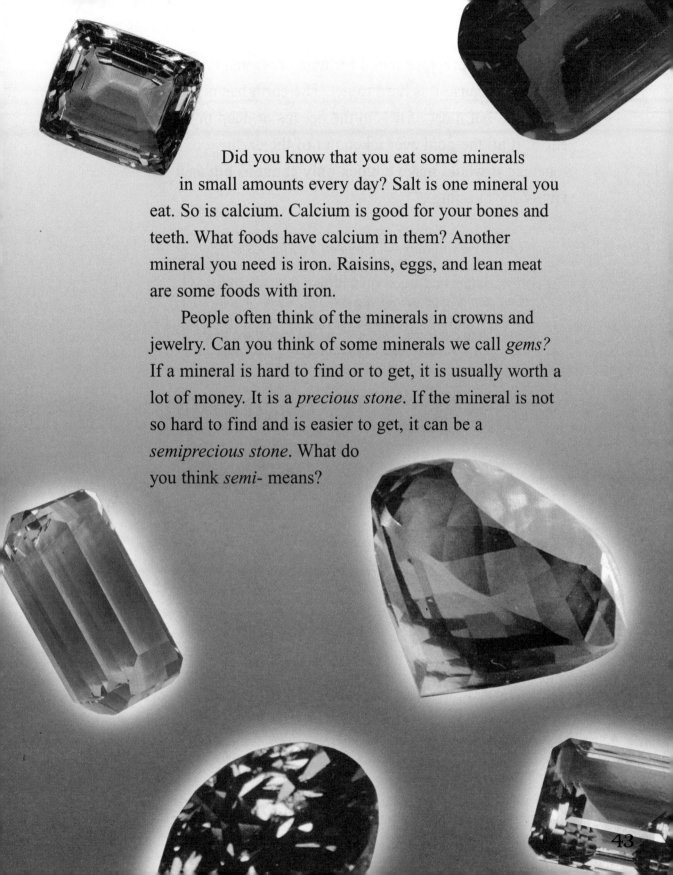

Did you know that you eat some minerals
in small amounts every day? Salt is one mineral you
eat. So is calcium. Calcium is good for your bones and
teeth. What foods have calcium in them? Another
mineral you need is iron. Raisins, eggs, and lean meat
are some foods with iron.

People often think of the minerals in crowns and
jewelry. Can you think of some minerals we call *gems?*
If a mineral is hard to find or to get, it is usually worth a
lot of money. It is a *precious stone*. If the mineral is not
so hard to find and is easier to get, it can be a
semiprecious stone. What do
you think *semi-* means?

Gold is a precious metal for many reasons. It is precious because it is hard to get. The earth has much gold in it, but most of it is in the oceans or deep in the earth. If all the gold ever taken out of the earth were put together, it would make a block only about as big as a five-story building.

> Gold is easy to work with. Melted gold (at 1,945°F; 1,063°C), when poured into a mold, will cool to room temperature and harden in less than thirty seconds. Gold can also be hammered very flat. A bar of gold about the size of a candy bar can be beaten thin enough to cover the walls of a gymnasium three times.

Finding Out...

About Iron

1. Get

five clear glasses
or test tubes

three cups of
strong tea

five labels

one-half cup each of orange juice,
pineapple juice, apple juice,
cranberry juice, and prune juice

2. Put about an inch of tea in each of the test tubes or glasses. Label each glass of tea with the name of a juice you will test.

3. Add an inch of juice to a glass of tea. Does the tea get cloudy? Record your observation. Add the other juices to the other test tubes of tea one by one. Watch for cloudiness.

4. If a fruit juice has the mineral iron in it, it will make the tea cloudy. Which juices have iron in them? Record your observations.

Rocks

Where do rocks come from? They certainly do not grow like plants. They are not born or hatched. Have all the rocks and stones that are around always been there?

Volcanoes make some of the rocks. When melted material from inside the earth cools, it becomes a kind of rock. It becomes *igneous rock. Igneous* means "fire." Why is that a good name for rock from volcanoes?

Some igneous rock looks like black glass. Some of it looks like sponge material. It has many small holes in it. When lava cools fast, not all the gases can get out of the molten rock. Why does that make holes in the rocks that form?

snowflake obsidian

Sometimes minerals are cemented together when they settle out of water. Rocks made this way are *sedimentary rocks*. Gravel, clay, and pebbles are sedimentary rocks. *Sedimentary* comes from a word meaning "to settle."

Other times, sedimentary rock comes from animal and plant remains. Shells and skeletons of sea animals break apart and then cement together to form limestone.

Chalk is a kind of limestone. Is there chalk in your classroom?

Soft coal is a sedimentary rock that comes from plants. The plants die and are covered with water. Then other materials fill in on top of the dead plants. The weight and heat of so much water and sediment turn the dead plants into coal. How do we use coal?

About Sediment

1. Get

sand   clay   water   many small   a quart jar
                                           pebbles   with a lid

2. Put the sand, pebbles, clay, and water in the jar. Leave some space at the top of the jar. Put the lid on tightly and shake the jar thoroughly.

3. Set the jar down and watch the sediment. What settles first? What takes the longest to settle? Record your observations.

A third kind of rock forms when igneous or sedimentary rock changes under heat and pressure. Rocks that change from one kind to another are called *metamorphic*. *Meta-* means "change." What do you think *-morphic* means?

Soft coal that stays under the ground will become hard coal. Hard coal not mined for fuel may become graphite. Where is graphite in your pencil?

Limestone can become marble. Marble is a rock that can be cut and polished. It is often white or gray, but it can also be other colors like pink, green, or black. The marble in statues was once limestone.

Artists like to use marble because it lasts and is beautiful.

Soil

Rocks, even huge ones, are slowly broken into little pieces by wind, rain, heat, cold, running water, and even plant roots. This breaking down of rocks is called *weathering*.

In places with lots of sand, wind can wear down rocks quickly. The wind blows the sharp pieces of sand against the rocks. The blowing sand becomes like sandpaper as it files away at the rocks. The grains that break away from the rocks are then carried by the wind.

Water also works on rocks, slowly wearing them down and carrying away the bits. Have you ever picked up stones from a shore or stream? How did they look? How did they feel? How were they different from stones in your school yard or beside the road?

Have you ever noticed how ice cubes stick up higher in the tray than the water did? Ice cubes stick up because water takes up more space when it freezes. Try to discover what that fact has to do with rocks wearing down.

Suppose it rains hard on some rocks. The water fills the cracks and pores in the rocks. Then the weather turns very cold. What will happen to the water? What will happen to the rocks?

Sometimes water runs under the rocks and into the ground. What do you think happens when that water freezes?

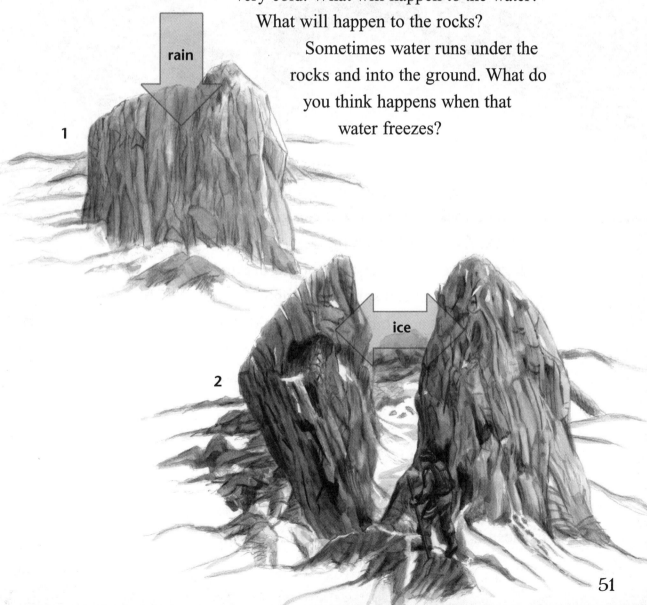

Plant roots seem much weaker than rocks, but they can split a rock. A seed or root can grow in a small crack in a rock. As it gets bigger, the seed or the root pushes with great force. It makes the crack wider and wider. Sometimes a plant can split a rock right in two.

When rocks are completely broken down, they make *soil*. When this soil mixes with the remains of dead plants and animals, it becomes the kind of soil plants can grow in.

The part of soil that is for growing is called *topsoil*. The soil below that is *subsoil*. It has many more pebbles than topsoil does. Why would subsoil have more pebbles than the soil on the top? There are no remains of plants in subsoil. Do you think plants could grow here?

When God created the earth, He gave it a rich topsoil. As man farms the land and mines it and builds on it, the topsoil is used up. Can you see how weathering is one way God makes sure there is always new soil? What would happen if no new soil formed?

Plant in Topsoil

Plant in Subsoil

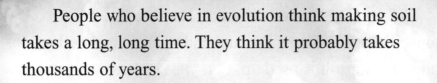

People who believe in evolution think making soil takes a long, long time. They think it probably takes thousands of years.

"The earth is the Lord's, and the fulness thereof; the world, and they that dwell therein."   Psalm 24:1

A few years ago when scientists looked at the ground around a volcano, they found that fourteen inches of soil had formed in only fifty years. Such observations show the earth is much younger than evolutionists say.

Animals Without Backbones

Some animals are called *invertebrates*. That name means that the animals have no backbones. Where would you find the animals pictured here?

The Tissue Animals

Some animals have cells formed into tissues, but they have no organs. The tissues form body walls just two layers of cells thick. Openings in the walls allow water to *circulate*—to move in and through—giving the animal food and oxygen.

One animal in this group is the sponge. For a long time, scientists called it a plant. Can you guess why? It looks like a plant. When not traveling through the water, it is attached to a rock. How do you think scientists came to know that it is an animal?

57

jellyfish

Other tissue animals also have hollow bodies. Their bodies have only one opening—the mouth—but they have waving fingerlike structures called *tentacles* around their mouths. Why do you suppose these animals have tentacles? Why do sponges not need tentacles?

The jellyfish, the sea anemone, the coral, and the hydra are all hollow-bodied animals with tentacles. Can you find the hydra on page 56?

sea anemone

coral polyps

The Worms

Worms are long, boneless, legless animals. This description might fit snakes except for one thing—what is that one thing?

There are three main groups of worms. Look at these worms. Can you guess how the three groups are divided?

Some worms are flat. These flatworms have three layers of cells. Most of these worms live on or in other animals.

Some worms have round, thin, smooth bodies that sometimes look like wire or thread. Hookworms and pinworms belong to this group.

Some worms have round bodies that are divided into *segments,* or rings. Earthworms and leeches are two such worms.

hookworm

earthworm

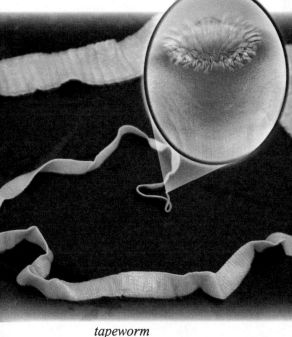

tapeworm

59

Finding Out... About Earthworms

1. Get

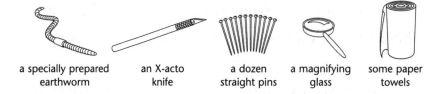

| a specially prepared earthworm | an X-acto knife | a dozen straight pins | a magnifying glass | some paper towels |

2. Look at the worm through the magnifying glass. How does its skin look? Can you see the segments, or rings, of its body?

3. Watch as your teacher dissects the earthworm.

4. Does the earthworm have a backbone? Did you find the worm's *crop,* the place where it stores food?

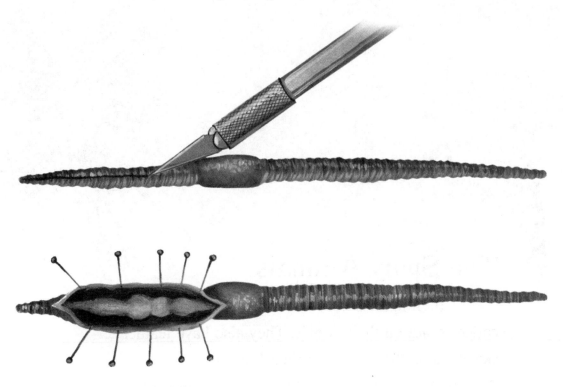

5. Draw an earthworm in your notebook.

starfish *sand dollar* *sea urchin*

The Spiny Animals

As their name says, spiny animals have tiny spikes called *spines* on their bodies. They also have leathery skeletons on the outside of their bodies.

What can you say about the shape of most spiny animals?

The Shellfish

The animals in this group have a confusing name. Although most of the animals in the shellfish group have shells, few of them are fish like the trout and the bass we usually think of. Some of them do not even live in the water! Shellfish are also called *mollusks*. *Mollusk* comes from a Latin word meaning "soft." Try to find out why an animal with a shell has a name that means "soft."

There are several kinds of mollusks. One kind is the hatchet-footed mollusk. It is a fleshy animal that lives inside two shells hinged by a muscle. Clams and oysters are in this group. Some clams in the South Pacific can grow to be four feet across!

Hatchet-footed mollusks have a muscular foot, shaped something like a hatchet, that the animal uses for digging. The muscle hinge is extremely strong. You probably could not open it with your fingers.

Where do you think we get the expression "to clam up"?

Digging into the sand and clamping its shells together are about the only ways a hatchet-footed mollusk can defend itself. Starfish can climb onto clams and oysters and pull at their shells until the mollusks tire and open up. Then the starfish eat the soft mollusks.

The *belly-footed mollusks* have one shell. The shells of these animals are usually shaped in a spiral. A snail is a belly-footed mollusk. It, like others in this group, has a muscular foot that puts out a kind of slime that helps move the animal along. People once thought this foot was part of the mollusk's stomach. Can you see how this group gets its name?

Some belly-footed mollusks live in the water. The conch, the abalone, and some snails, for example, live in the water. Slugs and some other snails, on the other hand, live on land.

Have you ever picked up a snail shell and looked inside it? How was it shaped? What might have happened to the snail?

slug

sea slug

snail

cuttlefish

octopus

Most *head-footed mollusks* do not have shells—at least not out where you can see them. The squid and the octopus have shells inside their bodies. Both animals have tentacles and sharp beaks for capturing and eating food.

Most squids are about three feet long. But some have grown to be almost sixty feet long. What would you do with a squid that big?

One head-footed mollusk, the nautilus, does have an outside shell. Unlike the hatchet-footed mollusks whose shells grow bigger as they do, the nautilus adds chambers to its shell. The chambered nautilus, as it is usually called, adds a new section to its spiral shell every year and moves into it, sealing off the old chamber.

Mollusks are useful animals. People eat clams, oysters, snails, abalone, and even octopuses and squids. We use the shells of these animals to make buttons, powder, chicken feed, and decorations. Certain oysters can also produce an expensive and beautiful gem—the pearl.

THIS CHAMBER CLOSED!

Sometimes an oyster sucks in a grain of sand or some other object that gets stuck under the shell. If the sand does not get washed out, the mantle (the tissue that makes the shell) grows smooth layers of shell around it. Over the years, the layers of shiny shell build up and form a pearl.

Sometimes a person may put a bead or a small bit of shell inside an oyster to make it form a pearl.

It still takes years to get a pearl large enough to use in jewelry.

The Arthropods

How is a grasshopper like a crab? *Arthro-* is a Latin word-part that means "joint." *Pod* comes from a Greek word meaning "foot" or "leg." What, then, do you suppose all arthropods have?

The *arthropods* are the largest group of animals. In this group is everything from shrimp to ants, from bees to butterflies, from lobsters to centipedes. There are more arthropods than all other living things put together.

hermit crab

scorpion

An arthropod has a skeleton on the outside of its body. The skeleton is not made of bone. It is made of *chitin,* a tough, sometimes transparent material. Because the skeleton is on the outside, it is called an *exoskeleton*. What do you think *exo-* means?

Not only arthropods have chitin on their bodies. The earthworm also has small bristles of chitin on its underside. These bristles are not feet but projections that give the worm traction. They work somewhat like spikes on an athlete's shoes.

All arthropods have *appendages*—parts that join to the body, like legs. These appendages have joints that bend. They are always paired. One side of an arthropod's body looks just like the other.

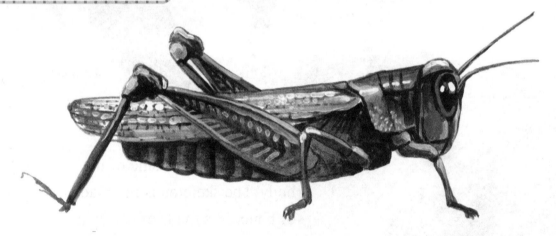

"Thy crowned are as the locusts, and thy captains as the great grasshoppers, which camp in the hedges in the cold day, but when the sun ariseth they flee away, and their place is not known where they are."   *Nahum 3:17*

The shrimp, the lobster, the crayfish, the crab, the pill bug, the water flea, and the sow bug are one group of arthropods. They are *crustaceans*.

Does it sound as if crustaceans might be rather crusty creatures? They are crusty in a sense. The word *crustacean* comes from a word meaning "shell." Every crustacean has a skeleton on the outside of its body that is shell-like and that has joints that bend. Crustaceans have at least five pairs of legs that are jointed.

lobster

crab

71

Crustaceans have two pairs of gills, which let them breathe underwater, and two pairs of feelers. The crustaceans live in fresh water or salt water. How are they like the mollusks? How are they different? Have you ever eaten any of these animals? Which ones?

Most crustaceans *molt:* they shed their skeletons and grow new ones. Crayfish, for example, molt seven times in their first year. Can you figure out why they need to molt? Why does the chambered nautilus make new chambers in its shell?

Some crustaceans eat dead animals. How does this way of feeding make them useful?

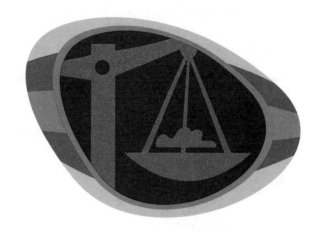

Mass and Weight

6

"A just weight and balance are the Lord's."

Proverbs 16:11

Have you ever heard someone say he would like to lose some weight? What he probably really wants to do is to lose some mass. *Mass* is how much "stuff" or matter is in something. *Weight* is how hard gravity pulls on something.

Mass

If you could figure out how much matter makes up an elephant, you could be sure that it would have that same amount of matter anywhere in the universe. Its *mass* would stay the same. If you took it to the moon, it would still have the same amount of matter in it. If you took it to Mars, its mass would be the same as on the earth. It would always have the same amount of matter.

Weight

The weight of that elephant, however, would be different if you took it to different places. It would be different on Mars from what it is on the earth. It would be different on the moon from what it would be on Mars.

Every object pulls or attracts every other object toward itself. The bigger the object, the more it pulls. The earth pulls on you, and you pull on the earth. But the earth is far bigger, so its pull is much greater.

The moon's gravity is less than the earth's. You weigh more on the earth than you would on the moon. If you weigh sixty pounds on the earth, you would weigh ten pounds on the moon. The elephant can weigh six tons on the earth. How much would it weigh on the moon?

EARTH

MARS

The measure of the pull of gravity on something is *weight*. The more gravity pulls on something, the heavier it is.

The gravity of an object always pulls things toward its center. The closer something is to the center of the object, the more gravity pulls on it. Where would you weigh a little more—flying in an airplane one mile above a desert or standing in the desert?

You would weigh less flying in an airplane than standing on a mountain. Why is that?

Which has more mass—a bicycle or a tractor? Which weighs more? Which weighs more—you or your science book? Which has more mass?

Can you say that objects of small mass usually weigh less than objects with more mass? Can you say that usually the more mass an object has the more it will weigh?

An astronaut out in space has no weight. He is "weightless." Does he have mass? Will his mass be the same on the earth? Will his mass be the same on the moon?

Weights from Old Times

The first time a weight is mentioned in the Bible is in Genesis 23:15. Abraham asks Ephron how much a piece of land is worth. Ephron says it is worth "four hundred shekels of silver." A shekel is about one-half ounce.

Six fruit Lifesavers weigh about a shekel. Ephron's land was worth about twelve and a half pounds of silver.

A talent equals 3,000 shekels. A talent was said to be as heavy as a load that a man could carry easily. Is this measure always going to be the same everywhere?

In England, 700 years ago, Henry III declared that a penny should weigh as much as thirty-two grains of dried wheat. Would this measure be likely to be more the same in every place than the Hebrew talent? Would a penny weigh the same all the time?

"And Abraham hearkened unto Ephron; and Abraham weighed to Ephron the silver."   *Genesis 23:16*

Each country, even each town, might have its own way of saying how heavy things were. How would this be a problem for people who traveled or tried to sell goods in different places?

Suppose that your class is divided into two "countries." Each has its own way of weighing things. One says a "tup" is the weight of six unsharpened pencils. The other says a "tup" is the weight of four unsharpened pencils. Which one is right? How would you tell someone from the other country how much something weighs?

Weights Today

Today the United States has important measures that are the same all over the country. A *pound* is sixteen ounces in every town, for example. A *ton* is 2,000 pounds. Still, some measures are not always the same. A ton of hay is measured by volume, not by weight.

In New Mexico, it takes a bigger stack of hay to make a ton than it does in Oklahoma.

Scientists use measurement standards that are the same everywhere. These standards make up the *metric system*. With this system, scientists measure mass in units such as *grams* and *kilograms*.

A paper clip has a mass of about one gram. A thousand paper clips would have a mass of about one kilogram. Can you guess what *kilo* means?

A newton equals about $\frac{1}{5}$ pound or about 3.2 ounces. If you weigh 60 pounds, you would weigh 300 newtons in the metric system.

Why do you think all scientists use the same system for measuring? How would they tell each other what they found out in their experiments if each used a different system of weights?

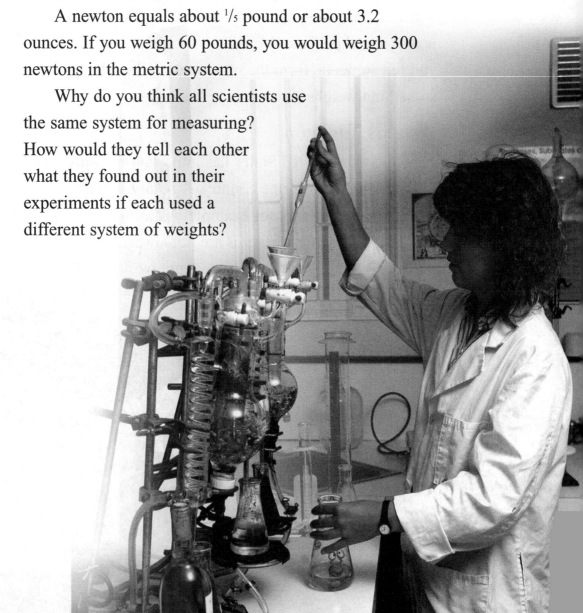

Weighing Machines

People have been weighing things for a long time. Almost 5,000 years ago the Egyptians used a *balance*. The balance was a bar across another bar.

This balance held a small pan on each side. When the crossbar was level, the weights in the pans were the same. How would you use this machine to find out how much a rock weighs? What would you put on the other side? You would have to use a weight you knew on the other side.

Today some scientists working with chemicals use this kind of balance. The balances they use are so carefully made that they can weigh a hair.

Some balances can even show the difference between the weight of a blank paper and a paper with words written on it!

Another kind of weighing machine is a spring scale. Have you ever weighed a letter in the post office? You probably used a spring scale.

A spring scale is just what its name says. It is a scale that works on a spring. The springs in some scales are above what they are weighing. When the spring stretches out, it measures weight.

Some spring scales have the spring under what they are weighing. When the spring is pushed down, it measures weight. The postal scales work this way.

Why Weigh Things?

Can you think of some reasons that people weigh things? What can the doctor tell about you by weighing you? Why do we buy food by weight? Why do trucks on the highway have to be weighed?

83

Finding Out... About Balances

1. Get

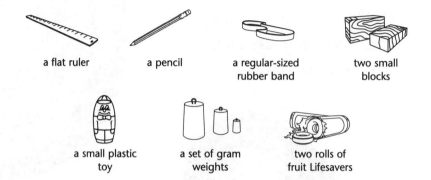

a flat ruler   a pencil   a regular-sized rubber band   two small blocks

a small plastic toy   a set of gram weights   two rolls of fruit Lifesavers

2. Put the pencil across the middle of the ruler. Slip the rubber band around one end of the pencil, over the ruler, and then around the other end of the pencil.

3. Place the two blocks about two inches apart. Lay the pencil across the blocks. Now you have a balance.

4. Put the toy on one end of the balance. How many Lifesavers does it take to balance the toy? Can you say about how many shekels would be needed?

5. Balance the toy with the weights. How many grams does it take to balance the toy?

Finding Out... About Weight

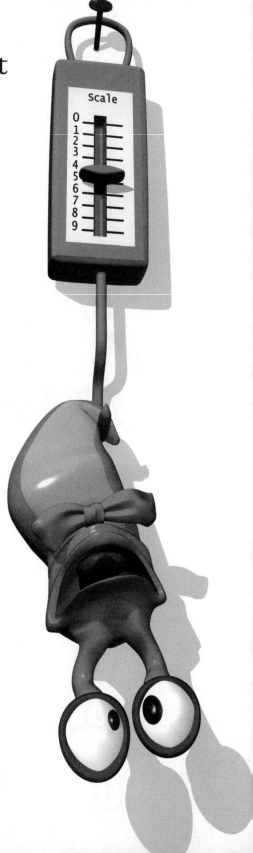

1. Get

a spring scale   several objects
to weigh

a plastic bag   your notebook
page

2. Hang the spring scale on a hook or a nail. Be sure the pointer is on zero.

3. Choose an object to weigh. If it cannot be hung from the scale, put it in a plastic bag and hang the bag from the scale.

4. Weigh each of your objects. Record the objects and their weights on your notebook page.

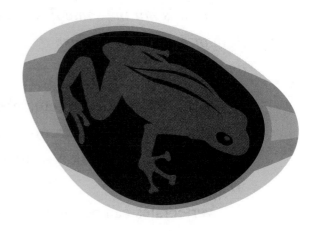

Animals with Backbones

"All flesh is not the same flesh: but there is one kind of flesh of men, another flesh of beasts, another of fishes, and another of birds."   *I Corinthians 15:39*

An invertebrate, you remember, is an animal without a backbone. The word part *in-* means "not" or "no." What then, do you think a *vertebrate* is? It is an animal *with* a backbone.

Vertebrates can be divided into groups. Each group has animals in it that have the same *characteristics*.

grey reef shark

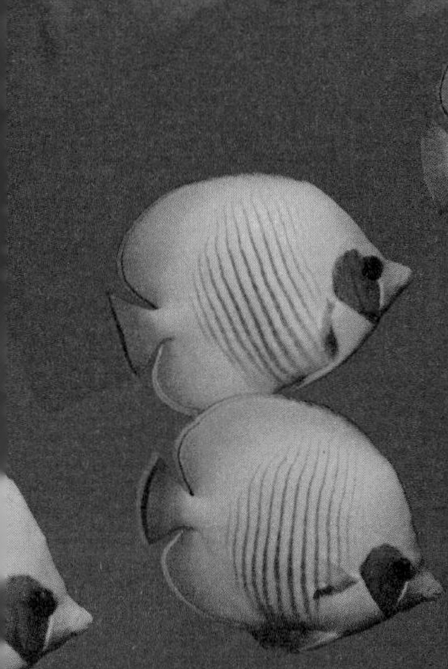

seahorse

Fish

How are these animals alike? They are all fish. Fish have structures called *gills* by which they take in oxygen. They also have *scales*. Fish hatch from eggs and live only in water, and they are cold-blooded. Their body temperature goes up or down with the temperature of their environment.

butterfly fish

trout eggs and fry

The archerfish has a clever way of getting its food. The archer lives in East India. It gets its name from the way it hunts. Can you imagine how a fish might be an archer?

> The archerfish shoots a jet of water out of its mouth to knock insects into the water. It can shoot a fly off a leaf on the riverbank or take a gnat out of the air. When the insect falls into the water, the archerfish swims over and eats it.

red-eyed tree frog

Amphibians

How are these animals different from fish? These animals are *amphibians*. *Amphibian* comes from *amphi-* ("double") and *-bios* ("life"). What could a name like "double life" tell about such an animal?

Amphibians hatch from eggs in the water. When they become adults, they usually live on land. They breathe with *gills* when they are young, but they breathe with *lungs* as adults.

Have you ever touched a frog or held a salamander? Amphibians have smooth, moist skin and are cold-blooded. What will happen to a salamander's temperature if it slides off a sunny rock into cold water?

spring salamander

Would you be surprised to find an animal called a mud puppy in the amphibian group? Sometimes it is called a waterdog. But it is not a puppy or a dog. It is a salamander.

The mud puppy can grow to be seventeen inches long. Its head looks a little like a dog's head. Its head gives it part of its name. Where do you think the rest of its name comes from?

The mud puppy's gills are purple. Its body is brown. And its tail is light orange. It lives in Canada and in the middle and eastern United States. Have you ever seen a mud puppy?

Finding Out...

About Amphibians

1. Look outside for a frog or a salamander. Where would be a good place to look?

2. If you can catch one, touch its skin gently. How does it feel? Put it back where you found it.

3. Record what you saw and felt.

Reptiles

A lizard looks like an amphibian, but it is not one. How can you tell a lizard from a newt? They look a lot alike. But a lizard belongs to a different group of vertebrates. A lizard is a *reptile*.

Reptiles are cold-blooded like amphibians. But they are different from amphibians in other ways. Reptiles usually hatch from eggs on land. Where do amphibian eggs hatch? Reptiles breathe with lungs. Why do you think reptiles can breathe with lungs right away but amphibians have gills? Reptiles have scales. What kind of skin does an amphibian have?

Can you think of any reptiles in the Bible?

iguana

boa

turtle

This reptile is a tuatara. It lives on an island near New Zealand. It is a one-of-a-kind reptile.

The tuatara has three eyes! It has an eye on each side of its head—and one right in the middle on the top. Scientists do not know for sure whether the top eye sees.

The tuatara hunts at night and sleeps in the day. It shares a burrow with a sea bird called a sooty shearwater. The shearwater eats during the day and sleeps at night. Can you see how the house-sharing works out? Reptiles usually eat eggs, but the tuatara does not touch the shearwater's eggs.

Birds

Birds are warm-blooded. They hatch from eggs on land. Do they breathe with lungs or gills? What do birds have that no other vertebrates have? Birds have feathers. Do you know what the largest bird in the world is? Does it have feathers? How big do you think an ostrich is? What is the smallest bird? How big do you think its eggs are?

red-tailed hawk

ostrich

hummingbird

The feathers of this bird are so grand that a long time ago they were used as money.

One of the most beautiful birds in the world is the bird of paradise.

One kind of bird of paradise has bright blue feathers on its head. Its neck is a rich yellow. The bird can raise its neck feathers to make a golden halo behind its head. Its breast is a deep green, and its back is a dazzling red. The long blue tail feathers end in a curl.

For all its lovely feathers, the bird of paradise makes a harsh sound, something like a crow's call. It eats fruit and insects. Do you think it lives in a jungle or a desert? Most of these birds live in New Guinea.

Mammals

Do you think these animals have anything in common? These animals are born alive. They give milk to their young. All of them have hair, breathe with lungs, and are warm-blooded. These animals are *mammals*.

What two groups of vertebrates are warm-blooded?

lemur

giraffe

rhinoceros

lion

A mammal you may not have heard of is the capybara. It belongs to the same family as mice and rats. It has stiff brown hair, but it has no tail.

This animal eats only plants. What word do scientists use to describe such an eater? It lives in South American jungles. What kind of plants do you think it likes to eat there? The capybara has webbed feet. Where do you think it spends a lot of time?

What kind of sound do you suppose it makes? It makes a sound like a bird. It goes "tweetle-tweet." Capybaras can grow to weigh almost two hundred pounds. Can you imagine an animal that big making such a small sound?

About Vertebrates

1. Get

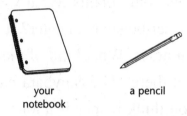

your
notebook

a pencil

2. Look at the pictures and read the descriptions below.

3. Record your answers.

This animal lays eggs on land. It has scales on its legs and neck. It is cold-blooded and breathes with lungs. Which group is a turtle in?

This animal is hatched from an egg in the water. Later it comes to live on land. It has smooth skin. It is cold-blooded. Which group is a frog in?

Although this animal has wings, it has no feathers. It has fur and gives birth usually to one young a year. What group does the bat belong to?

This animal puzzled scientists for years. It lays eggs and gives milk to its young. It has hair, is warm-blooded, and has webbed feet. It is a *platypus*. Which group do you think scientists finally decided to put it in? They put it in the mammal group. Can you give two reasons for calling the platypus a mammal?

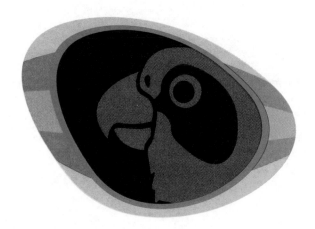

Birds

8

How Birds Look and Act

Do you know your state bird? If you live in Pennsylvania, it is the ruffed grouse. If you are from Minnesota, it is the common loon. If you are in Oregon, it is the western meadowlark.

Whatever your state bird is, it has some things in common with all other state birds. Can you think what some of these things are?

What do you think makes birds different from all other animals? Is it that they can fly? Bats fly, but they are mammals. Insects fly, but they are not birds. Besides, not all birds can fly. Do you know a kind of bird that does not fly?

Feathers

What do birds have that no other animals have? Feathers. Even birds that do not fly have feathers. Ostriches, for example, have many beautiful feathers. But the ostrich does not have the right skeleton for flying.

Each feather on a bird can be moved by a separate muscle. A bird can move its feathers to help itself get warm or to fly or to keep its balance on a perch.

Birds have to take good care of their feathers. Birds *preen* their feathers often. They rub them with their bills, or beaks. They wipe oil on them. Sometimes they take baths in water or dust. Why do you think birds are so careful about their feathers?

Flight

Do you think all birds fly alike? There are three main ways that birds fly.

Some birds *glide,* or sail along on moving air. Gliding birds hold their wings straight out and still most of the time. They ride up and down on winds. What gliding bird have you seen?

gliding

Other birds fly mostly by flapping their wings. With every flap, the wing does two things: part of the wing gives *lift* and part pushes forward. What flapping bird have you seen?

flapping

hovering

The hummingbird is the only bird that can really hover. It can stay in one place in the air. It can also fly backwards. To hover, a hummingbird moves its wings in the shape of the number 8.

106

Migration

Some birds fly long distances at the same times every year. This orderly movement to a different place is called *migration*. Not all birds migrate. Those that do seem to be able to find their way by the sun and stars.

Birds that migrate put on extra weight just before their travels begin. Why do you think they need to do that? Some birds double their usual weight.

Swallows, Canada geese, and arctic terns are some migrating birds. The terns are the champions. They fly almost 22,000 miles each year.

One bird, a bobwhite, ate 10,000 seeds in a day. What do you think of the phrase "eating like a bird" now?

Some scientists think weather and temperature changes tell birds when to migrate. Some think birds travel when the days get shorter or when the food becomes hard to find. How do you think birds know when to migrate?

"Doth the hawk fly by thy wisdom, and stretch her wings toward the south?"　　　　　　　　　　　　*Job 39:26*

Eggs

All birds hatch from eggs. Can you think of another animal that hatches from an egg? Some reptiles do. But bird eggs are different from other eggs.

Bird eggs are hard-shelled. Some have very thin shells, but the shells are strong. The shell lets air pass in and out. Inside the shell are the yolk and the *albumen*. The yolk is the food for the growing chick. The albumen gives the chick water and minerals. Are all the needs of the growing bird met?

A group of eggs in a nest is called a *clutch*. Eggs come in all sizes. A hummingbird egg is not much bigger than the end of your thumb. How big is a chicken egg? Most eggs are bigger on one end than the other.

What colors can chicken eggs be? Look at the picture of the eggs in the nest on this page. They are robin eggs. What color are they? Why do you think most birds that nest on the ground lay speckled eggs? How does the color help keep them safe?

Camouflage

Eggs are often kept safe by their color. Do you think birds can stay safe the same way? Can you see the bird in this picture? How does its color suit its living place? Hiding by blending in with what is around is called *camouflage*.

Where do you think this bird lives?

Usually the male bird has brighter, more colorful feathers than the female. Why do you think the female bird has colors that are not as easy to see?

Watching Birds

People who spend a lot of time trying to see many kinds of birds are *bird watchers*. Some people watch birds for a living. Some watch them for a hobby. Anyone can be a bird watcher. What do you think you need for watching birds?

Tools

Since some birds will not come close to people, bird watchers use binoculars. *Binoculars,* or field glasses, make things look bigger and closer. Have you ever looked through a pair of binoculars?

Another good tool is a *field guide,* a bird book. Guides have pictures and descriptions of many birds. They help you find the names of birds you have seen.

You can see birds by going out walking or hiking. You can also try to get birds to come to where you are. How do you think you could get birds to come to you?

Many people put up bird feeders. Different birds like different foods. Chickadees like sunflower seeds. Hummingbirds like sugar and water. Baltimore orioles like oranges. Almost all birds like cracked corn. How would you try to get one kind of bird to come more often than others?

Birds will also come to water to drink and to take baths. Some people buy birdbaths for their lawns. But even a garbage can lid filled with water can become a popular pool with birds. Robins especially like to take baths.

Finding Out...

About Birds

1. Get

birdseed

bread

plastic milk carton

scissors

several feet of string or cord

large needle

suet, meat scraps, dried apple slices, raisins

2. String the food on two- or three-foot pieces of cord. String at least one piece of each food.

3. Cut off the top half of the milk carton. Keep the bottom and run a string through each side. Fill the bottom with birdseed.

4. Hang the strings of food on tree branches. Hang the birdseed holder from another branch or tree.

5. Record how many birds come to your feeders. Do different birds come to each feeder?

Besides putting out food and water, you can bring birds in by hanging up birdhouses. Just as birds like different foods, they also like different kinds of houses.

Tree swallows like brown or gray houses near some water. Purple martins seem to like white houses put up on poles in open spaces. Chickadees like brown or tan houses near big trees.

Some birds need a perch at the hole of the birdhouse; some do not. Some birds like to live near buildings; some like to live at the edge of woods.

Suppose you wanted chickadees to live near you but not tree swallows. Where should you put the birdhouse?

Even if you do not have binoculars, a field guide, bird feeders, a birdbath, or a birdhouse, you can be a bird watcher. You need three things. Can you guess what they are?

You need your eyes, your ears, and your brain. Next time you go outside, be alert to the birds that may be near. Use your eyes. Look for flashes of color. Look for quick movements in the trees and in the sky. Use your ears. Listen for the songs and twitters coming from up on telephone poles or from deep in bushes and hedges.

Every good bird watcher writes down or tries to remember what he noted about the birds he saw. He tells where he saw the bird. He describes how the bird looked. He finds out, if he can, what the bird eats and where it nests.

Identifying Birds

Suppose you see a bird you have never seen before. How can you find out what it is called?

Do you know what kind of bird is pictured here? You can find out.

Size

Try to tell how big the bird is. Compare it to a bird you know. Is it smaller than a robin? Is it bigger than a wren? Does it seem to be an adult bird? Or is it a baby?

Color and Marking

Describe the colors you see. Tell where the colors are. Are the wings a different color from the head or tail? What color are its feet? What seems to be the main color of the bird?

Does the bird have spots or stripes anywhere? Look for patches on the wings or tail. For example, a male red-winged blackbird has a bright red patch on each shoulder.

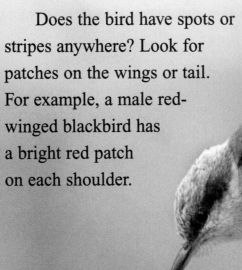

Shape

Is there anything about the bird's shape that makes it special? How long is its tail? Does its head have a *tuft,* a bunch of feathers that stick up? Is the bird sleek and slim or is it short-bodied? Does it have long wings or short ones?

Look at the bill if you can. Is it short and pointed or long and curved? Is it flat or cone-shaped?

Some beaks are made for cracking seeds. Some beaks are best for getting food from the water. Other beaks are for tearing prey.

Actions

Watch how the bird moves and what it does. Some birds are graceful. Swallows skim on the air like paper airplanes. Some birds are jumpy. Sandpipers run here and there, sometimes bobbing back and forth.

Some birds walk more than they fly. Some hop a lot. Some birds never seem to light on the ground. Some sit calmly on a branch and then take off suddenly. Others flit up and down the branch before they fly.

Does the bird stay by itself or does it keep with a group? Does it preen much?

Songs and Sounds

A few people can identify birds just by hearing them. Every kind of bird has its own song or sound. But it is always good to see the bird as well as hear it.

Try to describe the sounds the bird makes. Does it *trill,* make a fluttering sound? Does it cheep or whistle or call? Does it sound as if it is saying words? A bobwhite seems to say its name. So does a whippoorwill. Have you ever heard a chickadee? How did that bird get its name?

After you have observed as much as you can about the new bird, try to find it in a good field guide. Match the size, color, and shape to one shown in the book. Then find out if its actions and sound seem to match. The more you observe about the bird, the easier it will be to find out its name.

The mystery bird on page 115 is a nuthatch. Can you see how its shape makes it different from most other birds?

What birds are these?

One thing that tells it is a nuthatch is that it climbs down trees head first. Not many birds do that.

Work

Suppose your teacher told you to read five pages in your book. You read the pages and put down the book. Would you say that you had done a lot of work? A scientist would say that you had done some work. But he would not say that reading is work. He would say that turning the pages and putting down the book are work.

How do you think a scientist tells what work is? He calls lifting a box work, but not holding it up. He calls picking up a bat work, but not standing in the outfield. He calls writing a letter work, but not reading one. What must be happening for a scientist to say work is being done?

What Is Work?

For scientists to say work is being done, something must move. What makes things move? A push or a pull makes things move. A push or a pull is a *force*.

When a force makes something move, work gets done. If a toy falls off a bed, does work get done? Yes, it does, because gravity is a force that made the toy move.

A force can stop things that are moving. It can keep things moving. If a force stops movement, is work being done? No, when an object stops moving, work is no longer being done.

Look at the pictures. Which ones show work being done?

123

How Much Work Gets Done?

You now know that scientists say work is done when a ball is lifted. But how much work is done when you lift a ball? It depends on how much the ball weighs and how high you lift it.

To know how much work is done, you have to know how much force pushes or pulls an object and how far the object moves. If you multiply "how much" by "how far," you can measure work. If the ball weighs one pound and you lift it two feet, you do two foot-pounds of work.

FORCE × DISTANCE = WORK
1 pound × 2 feet = 2 foot-pounds

If the ball weighs two pounds, how much work would it take to lift it two feet?

Scientists measure work in metric terms. If your ball has a weight of one *newton,* one newton of force will cause the ball to speed up one meter per second.

The *meter* is a measure of how long something is or how far something moves. A meter is about three inches longer than a yard. If a ball weighing one newton is lifted one meter, one newton-meter of work is done.

The newton-meter has a special name. One newton-meter of work is called a *joule. Joule* sounds like *jewel.* Why do you think scientists say *joule* instead of *newton-meter?*

If a cooler weighs five newtons and you lift it one meter, how many joules of work have you done?

About Work

1. Get

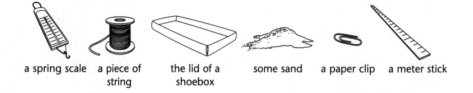

a spring scale   a piece of   the lid of a   some sand   a paper clip   a meter stick
             string   shoebox

2. Bend out the paper clip and push it through one end of the lid. Tie one end of the string to the paper clip.

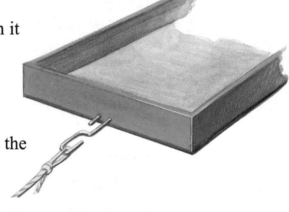

3. Tie the other end of the string to the hook on the spring scale. Put some sand in the lid.

4. See where the scale marker is when you can smoothly pull the lid. Put in sand or take out sand until the marker reads 200 grams.

5. Lay the meter stick on a table or the floor. Put the end of the lid with the paper clip even with the low-number end of the stick.

6. Pull the lid slowly until the same end of the lid is even with the far end of the stick. How many gram-meters of work have you done?

7. Take out sand until the scale marker reads 100 grams. Can you guess how far you will have to pull this load to do the same amount of work as before? Measure the distance and try it.

8. Record your observations.

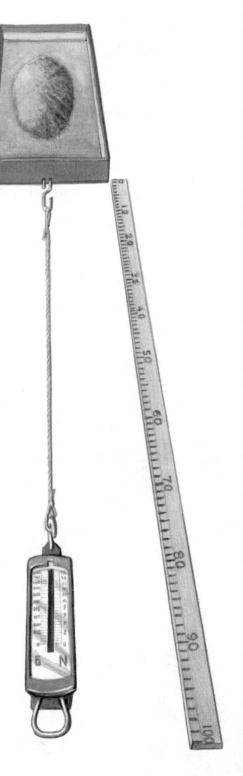

How Fast Is Work Done?

You can do work quickly or slowly. If it takes ten newtons of force to pull a sled for ten meters, you do 100 joules of work. If it takes you one minute to pull the sled, you still do 100 joules of work. If it takes two minutes, you are still doing the same amount of work.

But it is harder to work quickly than it is to work slowly. To show the difference between doing work quickly and doing the same work slowly, scientists talk about *power*. Power is the measure of how fast work gets done.

A long time ago a Scotsman named James Watt wanted to show how much power his steam engine had. He compared the work his engine could do with the work that horses can do.

Watt found that a horse can do 33,000 foot-pounds of work in one minute. An engine that can do that much work in a minute is a one-horsepower engine.

In the metric system, power is measured in *watts*. One watt equals one joule of work in one second. Where do you think the watt got its name?

Can you think of some engines that have the power of many horses? Can you think of something measured in watts?

Finding Out... About Power

1. Get

a 100-gram   a spring scale   a piece of   a stopwatch   a meter stick
weight   string

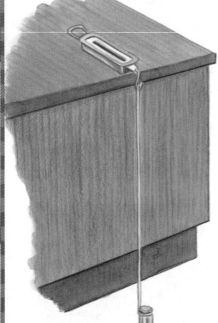

2. Tie one end of the string to the hook of the spring scale. Tie the other end to one 100-gram weight.

3. Put the weight on the floor. Lay the spring scale on the desk so that the hook is at the edge of the desk. Pull the scale slowly back. What does the scale marker read?

4. Measure the height of the desk. Record this height.

130

5. Pull the weight up to the edge of the desk in five seconds. How much work did you do?

6. Now pull the weight up in ten seconds. Did you do the same amount of work? Which pull took more power? Record your answers.

What Can Do Work?

Are people and horses and engines all that can do work? No, many things can do work. Look at these pictures. Can you tell what is doing the work in each one?

Moving air and moving water are other things that can do work.

Can you tell what is
doing or has done
work in these pictures?

Is this boy doing work? Why do you say so? What work have you done today?

"All thy works shall praise thee, O Lord; and thy saints shall bless thee. They shall speak of the glory of thy kingdom, and talk of thy power."

Psalm 145:10-11

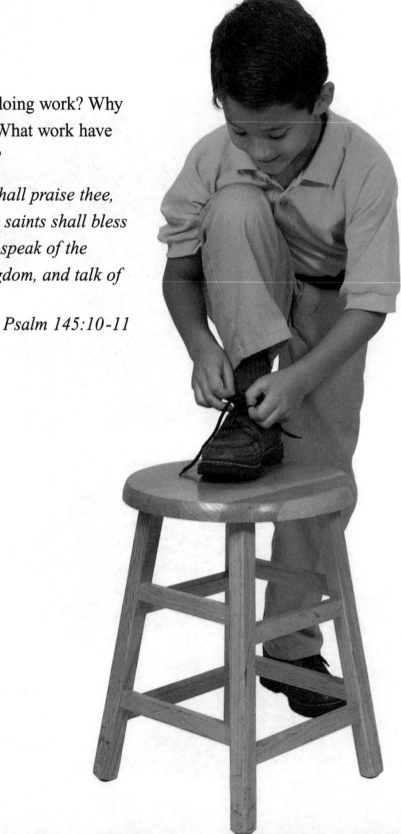

Skin

"Thou hast clothed me with skin and flesh, and hast fenced me with bones and sinews. Thou hast granted me life and favour, and thy visitation hath preserved my spirit."
Job 10:11-12

Look at the skin on your arm. There are many things you can notice about it. You can see its color. Is the skin on your arm all the same color, or are there places that are different from the rest of your arm? Feel the skin on your eyelid. Does it feel the same as the skin on the palm of your hand?

Look at the color and texture of the skin on your elbows (or someone else's). What can you tell about that skin? Look at the skin on your knuckles when your fingers are out straight. Now make a fist. What happens to the skin on your knuckles? Skin can fold and stretch.

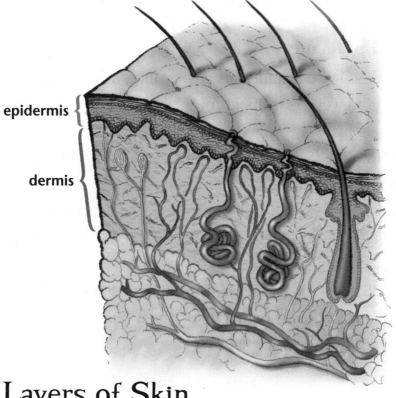

epidermis {

dermis {

Layers of Skin

Skin is an organ. Can you remember what an organ is? It is many cells and tissues working together. Skin has many parts, but it has two main layers.

The bottom layer is called the *dermis*. The word *dermis* means "skin." The top layer is called the *epidermis*. Which of the following meanings do you think the word part *epi-* has: "all," "on," or "two"?

Look again at your elbow. You may have noticed some loose white flakes of skin. (You may need to use a magnifying glass.) These flakes are dead cells from the top of the epidermis. Common things like your clothes and water help remove the dead cells. The living epidermis beneath is always making new cells to replace the old.

The Epidermis

Although the epidermis is very thin, it is strong enough to work as a shield for the body. This shield works in two ways.

How does your skin help you in the rain? How does your skin help you when you handle cleansers? Skin keeps out things that we do not need, like extra water. It also keeps out many things—like cleansers—that would do harm if they could get into the body.

What are some other harmful things that your skin keeps outside of the body? It keeps out *bacteria,* or germs. Why are germs harmful?

The epidermis also works like a shield by keeping inside the things that the body needs. One of the things that the body needs most is water.

Water keeps your body from drying out. It helps keep your body organs working and your blood flowing. It also helps your body stay the right temperature.

What do you think made the drops of water come out on this person's face? Has this ever happened to you? Were you too warm?

Finding Out...

About Cooling Off

1. Wet one of your hands with tap water.

2. Wave both hands in the air.

3. Record which hand felt cooler.

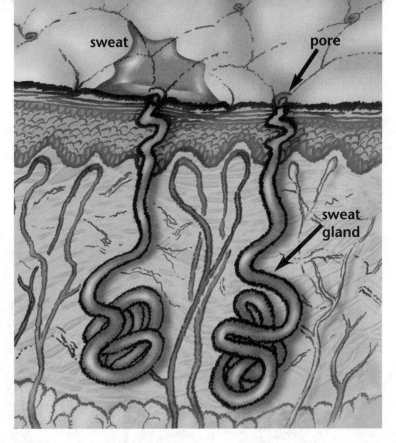

When you get too warm, more blood than usual comes to your skin. This blood is carrying heat from inside your body. When the blood reaches your skin, the *pores* open. Pores are tiny holes in your skin.

The heat leaves your body through the pores. At the same time, a mixture of water, salt, and a few other chemicals goes out of the pores. This mixture appears as drops on the skin. What do we call these drops? They are called sweat or *perspiration*.

When your skin is wet with perspiration, it feels cooler. What would happen on a cold day if you wore so many clothes that you perspired? You might get chilled. Your body would act as if the weather were hot outside, and you would cool off too much.

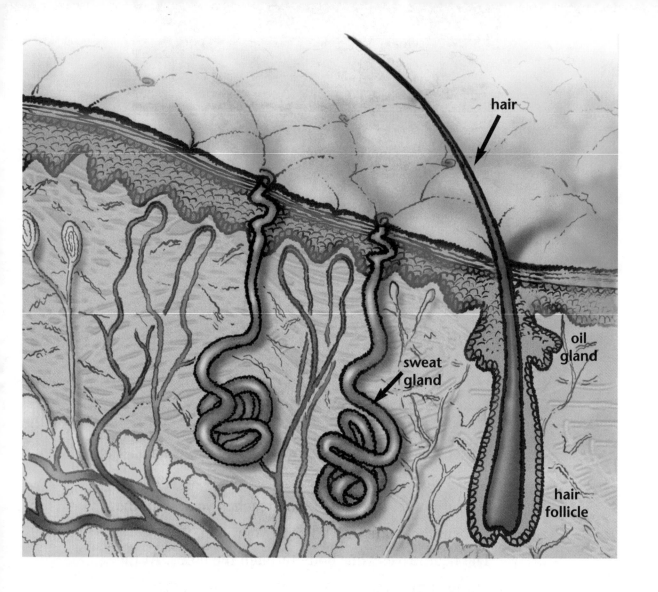

hair

oil gland

sweat gland

hair follicle

The special structures that move the water from inside the skin to outside the skin are called *sweat glands*. The top of the sweat gland is an opening. Do you remember the name of this opening?

Look at the bottom of the hair. Does the hair grow out of the epidermis or the dermis?

An oil gland is found in the skin at the base of the hair. Oil released on the skin helps protect the body. It helps keep the skin soft and "waterproof." It also protects the body from harmful things by trapping them until they can be removed. Oil also helps keep the skin warm.

The epidermis has many lines and grooves in it. If you look closely at your fingertips, you can see dozens of curved ridges. Everyone in the world has a different set of ridges on each of his fingers. They are called *fingerprints*.

The ridges on your fingertips help you pick things up. They help keep objects from slipping out of your grasp. They can also help identify people. When you were born, a nurse probably made your footprint or a handprint. Why do you think hospitals do that?

About Fingerprints

1. Get

an ink pad

a note card

a paper towel

2. Write your name on the card. Press your thumb on the ink pad and then on the note card.

3. Clean off your thumb. Compare your thumbprint with someone else's. Look at all the other thumbprints.

4. Record what you find out about the different ways thumbprints look.

The Dermis

The dermis is much thicker than the epidermis. It serves us in different ways. One way the dermis serves us is through the sense of touch. What are some ways you describe how things feel?

There are special structures in the dermis that let us know what things feel like. These structures are called *nerves*. If you did not have any nerves, you would not know how things feel.

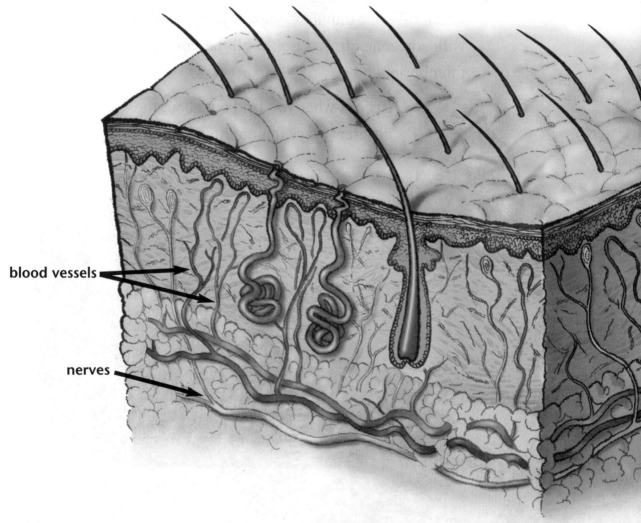

blood vessels

nerves

All of the body is covered by skin that has nerves in the dermis. But not all parts of the body have the same number of nerves. What part of the body do you use most often to touch things? Which part of the body would need the most nerves to tell you how things feel?

Inside the dermis are other structures called *blood vessels*. These structures move blood from place to place in the body. These blood vessels control how much blood goes to each part of the body. They can become wide and let a lot of blood come near the outside of the body. They can also become narrow and keep most of the blood near the inside of the body. When would the vessels get narrow to keep heat inside?

Can you think why there are no blood vessels in the epidermis? The smallest scratch would bleed if blood vessels were too near the top of the skin. Run your fingernail lightly across your hand. What happened?

On a warm day, should the blood vessels in the skin be wide or narrow? Which size opening would you want the vessels to have on a cold day?

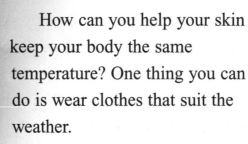

How can you help your skin keep your body the same temperature? One thing you can do is wear clothes that suit the weather.

Wear heavy clothing in cool weather. Heavy clothes will keep the cool air from reaching your skin. They will also keep your skin warm by trapping heat and keeping it near the body.

Wear light clothing in warm weather. Light clothes allow heat to leave the body because only a small amount is trapped. But wear enough clothing in warm weather to protect your skin from too much sun.

You can also help your skin protect the body by keeping your skin, hair, and nails clean. The skin with its grooves and oil can trap dirt. Use soap, water, and a clean washcloth to remove dirt. Soap and water remove more dirt than water alone does.

Your hair and nails also trap dirt in them. Shampooing your hair helps remove the dirt, oil, and dead cells. Your nails should be kept clean and should be cut properly.

Which objects in the picture above could hurt your skin? If you are careful with sharp objects, you can help your skin protect your body. Cuts in the skin can allow harmful things to enter your body. Cuts provide a deep place in the skin that can trap dirt and germs.

If you do get a cut, you should let it bleed a little. Then clean the cut with mild soap and water to remove dirt. You may need to put some germ-killing medicine on it, and you may need to cover it to keep dirt out. If a bandage is used, keep it clean and dry.

Cuts should be checked by an adult. Adults can help clean and cover cuts. They will also decide whether a doctor needs to check and care for your cut.

How
Plants Live

11

"For the earth which drinketh in the rain that cometh oft upon it, and bringeth forth herbs meet for them by whom it is dressed, receiveth blessing from God."

Hebrews 6:7

The plants in this photograph do not seem to be doing anything. Yet they are doing something very important. Only green plants do this. What do you think they are doing?

Making Food

Green plants are living things that are able to make their own food. Why do plants make their own food? Plants must stay in one place. A rabbit can hop from one place to another to get food. But a plant cannot get up and move to find food.

This process of making food is called *photosynthesis*. The word part *phot-* means "light." In the word *photosynthesis*, *-synthesis* means "put together." What do you think *photosynthesis* means?

The green parts of the plant are the places where food is made. Can you see the green "footballs" in this cell? They are *chloroplasts*. *Chloro-* means "green." The ending *-plast* means "small body." Can you see how these parts got their names? Chloroplasts are found only in cells that make up green parts of a plant. Where are chloroplasts not found?

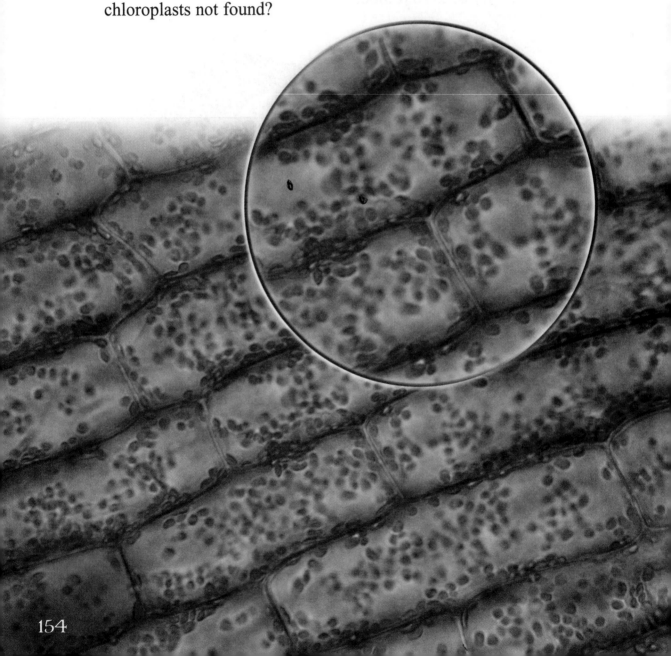

Incoming Materials

The materials that plant cells need to make food are called *incoming materials*. What do you think is one thing that plants need to make food? First of all, they need sunlight. Sunlight is one form of energy. When sunlight shines on the leaves and stems, they capture the energy. The cell stores this energy to use to make food.

A chemical called *chlorophyll* captures the sunlight energy. The ending *-phyll* means "leaf." What does *chlorophyll* mean? In what cells of a plant would you find chlorophyll? Chlorophyll makes chloroplasts green. Chloroplasts make the leaves and stems green. So what really makes a green plant green?

Green plant cells also need water. Water is carried from the roots to the stems and leaves in tubes. These tubes are long rows of hollow cells called *xylem*. Where do the roots get the water?

A third thing the green cells need is the gas *carbon dioxide* (CO_2). Carbon dioxide is part of the air that we breathe. How do you think the carbon dioxide enters the leaf?

The carbon dioxide gets into the leaf through small openings called *stomata*. These stomata are located on the underside of the leaf. The word *stomata* comes from a word meaning "mouth." Can you guess why we use the word *stomata*?

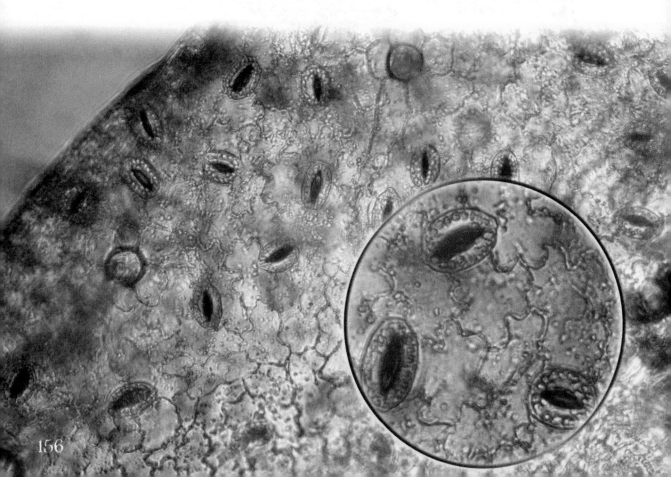

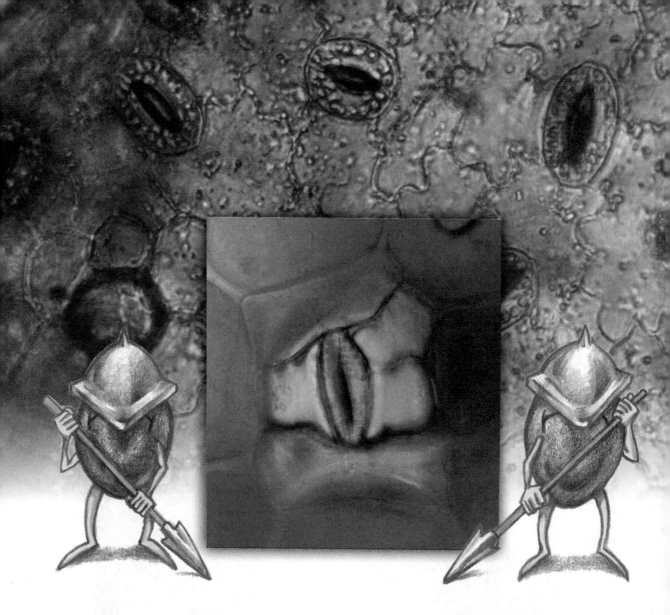

Two cells control the entrance to these mouths. They are called *guard cells*. They open and close like gates, letting in carbon dioxide.

Guard cells do two jobs. Besides letting in carbon dioxide, they also help make food. How can you tell? Can you find the chloroplasts in the guard cells pictured above?

Outgoing Materials

A plant takes the incoming materials—water and the carbon dioxide—and puts them together by photosynthesis to make *outgoing materials*. You have learned one of these already—food. But what is this food?

The food that plants make is sugar. This sugar made during photosynthesis moves out of the green cells and into the food-carrying tubes, called *phloem*. These tubes carry the sugar to different parts of the plant.

Another outgoing material is a gas called *oxygen*. The oxygen goes out of the cells through the stomata and into the air. Besides giving us food, how are plants helpful to people?

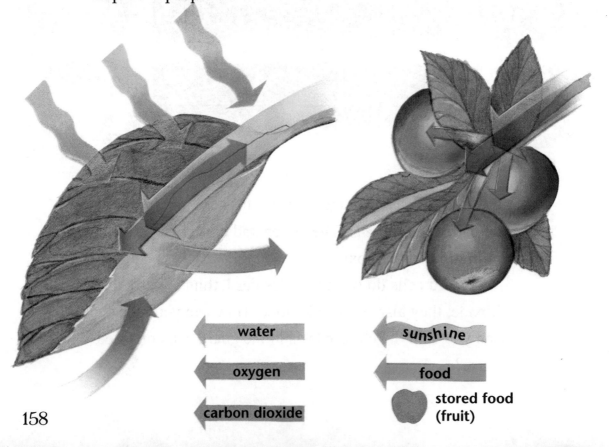

water

oxygen

carbon dioxide

sunshine

food

stored food (fruit)

The picture below shows the food-making process, *photosynthesis*. A plant gets energy from the sugar it makes. This energy helps the plant grow.

EARTH

Plants produce more food (sugar) and oxygen than they need. Sometimes the extra sugar goes to the stems and roots. Here it is stored as *starch*. Can you think of a root or a stem that people eat?

Sometimes the sugar is stored in the fruits growing on the plant. Name some sweet-tasting fruits.

Finding Out... About Xylem

1. Get

a stalk of celery   a glass   some water   red food coloring

2. Fill the glass half full with water. Add a teaspoon of food coloring. Put the celery into the water and leave it a day or two.

3. Take the celery out. After your teacher cuts the stalk, look at the parts that have turned red. What are these parts? What do they do for the plant?

4. Record how the celery looks. Why does it look that way?

Living things need energy for all of their activities.
People get energy from the food they digest.

Are the plants in this picture using energy? How are
the children using energy? How do you use energy?

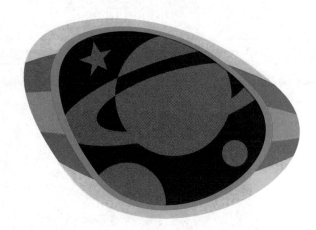

The
Solar System

CHAPTER TWELVE

Look up into the sky on a clear night and what do you see? You see the moon, perhaps, and planets and stars and stars and stars. How many stars do you think you can see?

You can see about 3,600 stars just by looking up.

For a long time men thought there were no other stars than the ones they could see on a clear night.

Then a man named Galileo took some pieces of curved glass and a metal tube and made an eyepiece that showed him stars no one had ever seen before. Galileo had made a telescope.

Since then people have been looking through more and more powerful telescopes at more and more stars and moons and planets. Scientists have seen a star with their telescopes that is billions and billions of miles away. And even that is not the edge of the universe.

When God created the heavens and the earth, He made something so vast and so wonderful that man can neither find out nor imagine all of it. Scientists with their telescopes and space probes have found out a few things about our part of the universe, our *solar system*.

Solar comes from a Latin word that means "sun." Since the planets move around the sun, the sun is the center of our small part of the universe. *System* comes from a word that means "to make stand together." What do you think the gravity of the sun does to the nine planets around it?

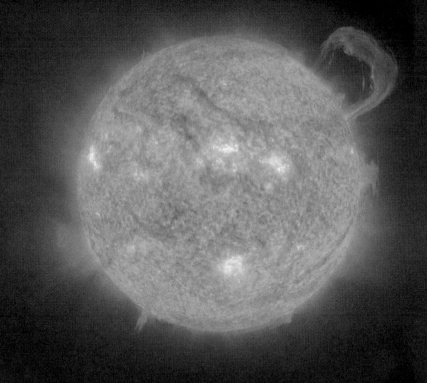

The Sun

The sun has more mass than any other object in our solar system. If you took everything else in the solar system—the planets, the moons, the comets, the meteors—and dropped them into the sun, it would be something like dropping a raisin into a basketball.

The sun is a star. Imagine yourself out in space, millions of miles from our solar system. As you look out the window of your spaceship, our sun looks like a small pinprick of light. It looks like one of the dimmer stars you used to look at when you were on the earth. The sun looks big from the earth because it is much closer to the earth than any other star.

If you could build a spaceship that could travel to the sun in 400 days, it would take you 800 years to get to the next star.

165

The Planets

The sun is the center of our solar system. The planets go around the sun in their orbits. There are nine planets that we know of, but some scientists think there may be others.

Saturn

Mercury

Earth

Neptune

the Sun

Mars

Venus

Uranus

Jupiter

Pluto

Mercury

The planet nearest the sun is Mercury. It is a planet that is both too hot and too cold at the same time for anything to live there.

Mercury turns very slowly on its axis. Our Earth turns once every twenty-four hours. Mercury turns once every fifty-eight Earth days! One day on Mercury is almost two months long. The side facing the sun gets up to 327°C (620.60°F) during that long day. The dark side falls to -183°C (-297.40°F).

Even though the days are long on Mercury, the years are short. Mercury travels around the sun in eighty-eight Earth days. About how many Mercury days are there in a Mercury year?

Mercury is bright, but we usually cannot see it because the sun is so much brighter. Mercury is small, just a little bigger than Earth's moon. It has no moon, or *satellite*, of its own. Why do you think that is so?

Venus

When anyone looks at Venus, even with a telescope, he never really sees the planet itself. He can see only the thick clouds all around it. The clouds are made of drops of acid.

Sometimes Venus is called Earth's sister. Venus is just a little smaller than Earth. Some space probes have sent back pictures of the surface of the planet. Venus has plains, volcano craters, mountains, and valleys. Some of its mountains are higher than any on Earth. But Venus has no water, and the clouds keep the temperature at 480°C (896°F). Is there any chance of finding life there?

The clouds around Venus reflect light well. They make Venus the brightest planet. Sometimes it is called the "morning star" or the "evening star."

> Venus rotates on its axis every 243 Earth days. It travels around the sun in 225 Earth days. Which is longer—a Venus day or a Venus year?

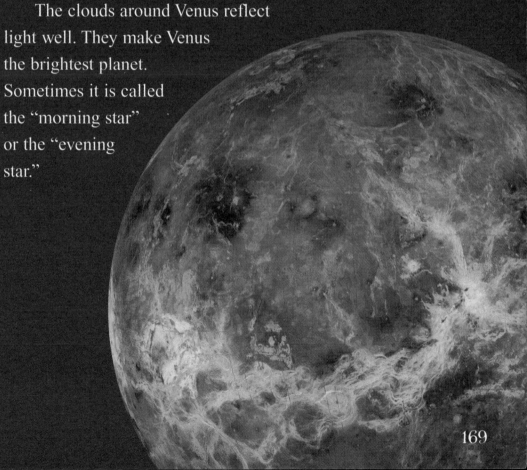

Earth

Earth is the third planet from the sun. It has water and an atmosphere (mostly oxygen and nitrogen) that is good for living things. Earth is the only planet that can have life on it.

the moon

Earth is ninety-three million miles from the sun. It spins on its axis once every twenty-four hours. It goes around the sun in 365 $\frac{1}{4}$ days.

Earth has one moon. The moon pulls the great waters of the oceans in tides. It reflects light at night, and it has been used to help men make calendars. The moon revolves around the earth every 29 $\frac{1}{2}$ days.

People used to have funny ideas about what holds Earth in place. The Egyptians believed Earth sits on five pillars. The Chinese thought elephants hold it up. But the Bible told us long before telescopes and space travel that Earth hangs on nothing.

"He stretcheth out the north over the empty place, and hangeth the earth upon nothing."   *Job 26:7*

Mars

Compared to Earth's cool blueness, Mars is a hot orange-red. Scientists believe that wild winds whip the red dust of the surface into the clouds we see.

Mars is about half the size of Earth. It has two moons named *Phobos* and *Deimos*.

The atmosphere on Mars has no oxygen and cannot block out meteors or harmful rays of energy. Because the atmosphere is thin, heat does not stay on the surface. It is usually about -30°C (-22°F) on Mars.

Mars turns on its axis every 24 ½ hours. What other planet has a day about that long? It goes around the sun in 687 days. About how many Earth years is that?

Jupiter

Jupiter

Jupiter is the biggest planet. It is about eleven times bigger than Earth. If Earth were the size of a pea, Jupiter would be about the size of a golf ball.

Do you think Jupiter is able to hold more than one moon in orbit? Jupiter has at least sixteen major moons. Galileo saw four of them through his telescope and named them Ganymede, Callisto, Io, and Europa. Ganymede and Callisto are bigger than Mercury. Io has erupting volcanoes. Europa is covered with ice several miles thick.

Jupiter spins faster than any other planet. It turns on its axis about every ten hours. If you could walk on Jupiter, you would feel as if you were walking on a merry-go-round because the planet spins so fast. But it takes twelve Earth years to go around the sun.

Jupiter is covered with thick, heavy gas and has many colorful bands of clouds across its surface. The bands shift and waver and sometimes change colors. There is one giant red spot on the planet that never seems to move. Scientists think that it is a great pool of swirling gas. The red spot is as big as Earth.

Io

Great Red Spot

Europa

Ganymede

Callisto

Encleadus

the rings

Saturn

Saturn is the planet known for its rings. It is almost as big as Jupiter. Its rings are made of ice and rocks traveling around the planet. Some pieces of the ice and rock are as small as dust. Some pieces are as big as a school building. Some people think that Saturn is the most beautiful planet because of its glistening rings.

Saturn has many moons. The largest one is called Titan. *In an old Greek story, Titans were giants who had great strength. What does this name tell you about Saturn's moon?*

Iapetus

Titan

A Saturn day is only 10 ¼ hours. What other planet has such a short day? Saturn takes 29 ½ Earth years to go around the sun. It is 887 million miles from the sun. Do you think its temperature is high or low? At the top of its clouds, Saturn has an average temperature of -140ºC (-220ºF).

Tethys

Dione

175

Uranus

Uranus gives off a pale green color. That color comes from the gases that are around the planet. Uranus also has rings, but they are not so bright nor so big as Saturn's.

Uranus spins on its axis in a way no other planet does. Other planets spin with only slight tilts away from the sun. Uranus spins like a top on its side. It turns on its axis in about eleven hours, and it travels around the sun once in eighty-four Earth years.

We know that Uranus has at least five moons. All of them are smaller than our moon. If you had to think up names for them, what would you call them?

Uranus is 1,780 million miles from the sun. Do you think it is warmer or colder than Saturn?

Neptune

If Earth were the size of a pea, Neptune would be the size of a grape. It is covered with ice and looks blue. The temperature is about -215°C (-355°F) on Neptune.

Neptune's day is about eighteen hours long. Its year lasts 165 Earth years. Imagine how long you would have to wait for your birthday on Neptune!

Pluto

Pluto is a tiny, slow, cold planet at the far edge of our solar system. It is about half as big as Earth. One day on Pluto is 7 1/2 Earth days long. How does its turning speed compare with the speeds of other planets?

Pluto is probably coated with ice, and the temperature there is probably about -230°C (-382°F). It is 3,660 million miles from the sun. It orbits the sun once in every 248 Earth years. How long would it take you to get to be nine years old on Pluto?

Finding Out...

About the Planets

1. Get

a softball

two large (0.8 mm across) grains of sand, three small (0.4 mm across) grains of sand

two heads of long dress-maker's pins

one small (7.5 mm across) pea, one large (9 mm across) pea

nine wooden stakes

a wide felt-tip marker

transparent tape

a measuring tape

2. Put the name of one planet on each stake. Tape the small grains of sand to the Mercury, Pluto, and Mars stakes. Tape the large grains to the Venus and Earth stakes.

3. Find an area outside where you can make a straight line about 370 meters (400 yards) long. Put the softball next to the school building to represent the sun.

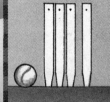  

4. Measure 3 ½ meters from the sun and push the Mercury stake into the ground. Measure 3 meters from the Mercury stake and push in the Venus stake.

5. Measure 3 meters from the Venus stake and push in the Earth stake. Measure 5 meters more and put in the Mars stake.

6. Measure 34 meters. Push in the Jupiter stake and tape the larger pea on top of it. Measure 41 meters and push in the Saturn stake. Tape the smaller pea on top of it.

7. Measure 90 meters from the Saturn stake and push in the Uranus stake. Tape a pinhead on top of it. Measure 50 meters and push in the Neptune stake. Tape a pinhead on top of it. Measure 140 meters and push in the Pluto stake.

8. Walk back to the "sun." Can you see Pluto from the sun? Can you see any of the "planets"? Walk out to "Pluto." Can you see the sun? Record your observations.

Asteroids

Asteroids are what some scientists call "minor planets." *Aster* means "star" and the *-oid* ending means "like." What do you think *planetoid* means? Sometimes the minor planets are called planetoids.

Asteroids are found mostly between Mars and Jupiter. Some are one hundred miles across, and some are no bigger than a baseball. Some are red and some are black. They are made of rock and metal. There are about 3,000 that we can see with telescopes.

Some scientists think that the asteroids are what is left of a planet that blew up. Others think they may be parts of another body, like a moon, that slammed into a planet and broke apart. No one can say for sure how God formed the asteroids.

Suppose you discovered an asteroid. What would you name it?

Comets

Comets are sometimes called "hairy stars." Can you see why?

Comets have a *head* and sometimes a *tail*. The head is made of ice and rock. Some comet heads are as big as our Earth. The solid part of the head is clouded about by frozen gases.

Comets have tails only when they come near the sun in their orbits. Can you guess why that is so? When a comet is near the sun, the frozen gases melt and become vapors that stream away from the head. Sometimes the tail of a comet can be one hundred million miles long. Where do you think the comet is when its tail is the longest? What happens to the tail when the comet goes away from the sun?

Most comets are yellow or blue, but some have been orange or pale green. Some comets come by the earth again and again over the years. The most famous comet is Halley's Comet. It has been seen every seventy-five or seventy-six years for the last two thousand years. It was last seen in 1986. When will it probably show up again?

Meteors

Have you ever seen a "shooting star"? You may have been out looking at the night sky when suddenly it seemed as if one of the stars fell out of its place and streaked downward. Although it was bright, it was not a star. It was a *meteor*.

Meteors are huge masses of rock or metal that travel through space. If it has an orbit around the sun, we call it a *meteoroid*. When a meteor comes through the gases that protect our earth, it heats up. Then it gives off light that we can see. Most of the time meteors burn up before they ever fall to the earth.

But once in a while, a really big meteor sails right on down to the earth. If it hits the ground, we call it a *meteorite*. Bits of the meteorite sometimes scatter around.

> Some meteorites are big enough to make a big hole called a crater in the earth. A large meteorite crater is in Arizona. It is 1,200 meters across and 180 meters deep. It struck the earth with the force of thirty million tons of exploding dynamite.

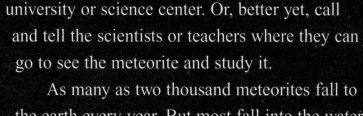

university or science center. Or, better yet, call and tell the scientists or teachers where they can go to see the meteorite and study it.

As many as two thousand meteorites fall to the earth every year. But most fall into the water. As they come through our atmosphere, they blaze white, blue, yellow, green, orange, or red.

183

Think of all the beautiful colors God has put in our universe. There are shining red, green, and blue planets, and bright red, yellow, and white stars. Even the tiny meteors flash with color. Then think of how orderly everything is. The planets go around the sun. The moons go around the planets. The whole solar system travels through space at an incredible speed.

And yet all things hold together. God has created everything in beauty and harmony. He maintains everything with exactness and careful watchfulness.

Our Earth is just a tiny dot in our solar system. Our solar system is only a small part of a great *galaxy*. Our galaxy is but one of the thousands and thousands of galaxies in the universe. It is no wonder the psalmist says, "What is man, that thou art mindful of him?" (Psalm 8:4)

"By the word of the Lord were the heavens made; and all the host of them by the breath of his mouth. He gathereth the waters of the sea together as an heap: he layeth up the depth in storehouses. Let all the earth fear the Lord: let all the inhabitants of the world stand in awe of him. For he spake, and it was done; he commanded, and it stood fast." Psalm 33:6-9

Reduce, Reuse, Recycle

Genesis 2:15 "And the Lord God took the man, and put him into the garden of Eden to dress it and to keep it."

God put Adam in the Garden of Eden so that Adam could take care of it. Adam was a steward—a keeper of God's creation. When Adam and Eve sinned, God had to send them out of the Garden of Eden. But God still planned for man to be the steward of His creation.

God has provided many resources, or things for us to use. However, we should be wise in the ways that we use those resources. We should not be wasteful.

Reduce

One way we can be good stewards is to reduce, or limit, the things we use. We can save gasoline in our cars by walking or riding a bike instead of driving. When we turn off lights that are not being used, we save electricity. Another way to reduce is by not buying things that we don't really need.

 Reuse

Another way to be a good steward is to reuse things. Reuse means to use things over and over again. Families often reuse clothing. A boy wears a pair of pants. When he outgrows the pants, the pants are given to someone else to wear. We can reuse paper by writing on the back of it instead of just the front. Sometimes items can be reused in a different way. Old shirts that cannot be worn anymore can be turned into paint shirts. Old towels can be reused as rags.

Recycle

Recycle means to use old material to make new items. Perhaps you have collected and sold aluminum cans. These cans are then recycled into new aluminum cans.

The plastic we recycle is made into many things, including carpet. Newspapers and other papers can be recycled and used to make more paper. We save resources when we recycle.

God expects us to be good stewards of what He has given us. Reducing, reusing, and recycling in your home and school are ways to take care of God's earth.

Useful Terms

absorb To take in.

amethyst A purple or violet form of quartz used as a gemstone.

amoeba A one-celled animal.

amphibian An animal that spends some of its life in the water and some on land. Amphibians hatch from eggs in water. They breathe with gills when they are young and with lungs when they are adults.

anvil One of the three small bones in the middle ear that carry sound to the inner ear.

appendage A projection, such as an arm or leg.

arthropod An animal with jointed legs, an exoskeleton, and a body made up of two or three parts.

asteroid A minor planetary body that revolves around the sun.

belly-footed mollusk A shellfish with one spiral shell that it carries on its back.

botanist A scientist who studies plants.

braille A system of raised dots that allows a blind person to read with his fingertips.

camouflage Hiding by naturally blending in with surroundings.

cell The smallest independently functioning living part of any living thing.

chlorophyll The substance in plant cells that makes plants green and uses sunlight to make food energy from water and carbon dioxide.

circulate To move in and through.

cochlea The spiral-shaped part of the inner ear from which sound messages are sent to the brain.

cold-blooded Having body temperature that changes along with the temperature of surroundings.

comet A small body that orbits the sun and has a bright head and a long, bright tail.

crater A large hole in the ground—usually bowl-shaped.

crustacean A type of animal with a hard outer covering on its body, such as a crab or lobster. Most crustaceans live in the water.

crystal A solid that has regular angles and sides that repeat to form a pattern.

customary measurement The system of measurement that includes inches, feet, and yards as well as cups, quarts, and gallons.

cytoplasm The jelly-like fluid that surrounds the nucleus of a cell.

deciduous tree A tree that loses its leaves in the winter.

dermis The bottom layer of skin, which contains nerves and blood vessels.

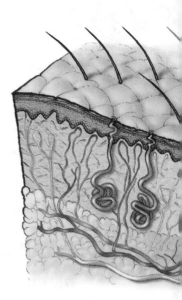

diamond A very hard, clear crystal that is made of pure carbon. Diamond is the hardest natural substance known.

eardrum The thin layer of tissue that separates the middle ear from the outer ear.

echo A sound that is heard again because it is reflected from a surface.

epidermis The top layer of the skin.

evergreen tree A tree that remains green all year.

force A push or pull.

galaxy A very large group of stars held together by gravity and rotating around a center.

gravity The force that pulls objects to earth and gives them weight. Every planet has gravity.

hammer One of the three small bones in the middle ear that carry sound to the inner ear.

head-footed mollusk A shellfish that does not have a visible outside shell, such as a squid or octopus.

herbivorous Eating plants and plant parts only, not meat.

igneous Formed by fire and great heat. Metamorphic rock is formed from molten rock, often from volcanoes.

inner ear The innermost part of the ear in vertebrates. The inner ear includes the cochlea and the nerve around it that sends messages to the brain.

invertebrate An animal that has no backbone.

mammal A warm-blooded vertebrate that breathes with lungs, bears live young, gives milk to its young, and has hair.

mass Substance; the amount of matter in an object.

membrane The soft, thin covering of a cell.

metamorphic Relating to a change from one kind to another, such as metamorphic rock.

metamorphosis A change, especially the shape changes some animals go through during their natural development.

meteorite A piece of matter that falls from space and strikes the earth's surface.

metric system A system of weights and measures based on the number ten. The meter is the basic unit in the metric system.

middle ear The part of the ear between the eardrum and the inner ear.

migrate To move in orderly fashion to a different place at certain times of the year.

mollusk A shellfish with a soft body.

nucleus The control center of a cell.

observe To watch or see.

omnivorous Able to eat both plants and animals.

orbit The path a heavenly body or artificial satellite follows as it moves around another, held by its gravitational pull.

organ A group of tissues working together.

outer ear The part of the ear outside the eardrum. The outer ear funnels sound into the ear.

perspiration Sweat.

phloem The food-carrying tissue of a plant.

photosynthesis The process by which a plant makes food using sunlight.

pitch The highness or lowness of a sound.

quality The distinguishing character or nature of something.

reflect To bounce back.

reptile A cold-blooded animal that has a backbone and scales and breathes with lungs. Most reptiles lay eggs.

scavenger An animal that eats dead animals.

sedimentary Made of matter settled out of water. Sedimentary rock is formed by minerals or animal or plant remains cemented together when settled out of water.

solar Having to do with the sun.

solar system A star and all the planets and other heavenly bodies that orbit it. Specifically, the sun and its planets.

stirrup One of the three small bones in the middle ear that carry sound to the inner ear.

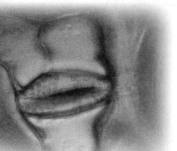

stoma A small opening in a plant through which it gets carbon dioxide.

telescope An instrument for observing distant objects close up.

tentacle A long, flexible arm of an invertebrate animal, used for grabbing and moving.

topsoil The top layer of soil, which is especially good for plants to grow in.

trill A fluttering call, like that made by some birds.

tuft A clump of grass, hair, feathers, or other similar material growing close together or held together at one end and free at the other.

vertebrate An animal that has a backbone.

vibrate To move rapidly back and forth.

warm-blooded Having a body temperature that stays the same, regardless of the surrounding temperature.

weathering Changing or breaking down from exposure to the sun, wind, rain, and other elements.

weight Heaviness; how heavy something is; the force of gravity on an object.

xylem The water-carrying tissue of a plant.

Index

Illustration Credits

Matthew Bjerk 13, 25 (top), 44, 57, 59, 67, 82, 86 (right), 99, 114, 120, 125, 139, 164, 171, 183
Paula Cheadle 2
Michael Cory Godbey 186-87
James Hargis 9, 15 (bottom), 25 (bottom), 47, 84 (bottom), 85, 126 (bottom), 127, 130 (bottom), 131, 158, 159, 166-67, 178-79 (bottom)
Deborah King 8, 15 (top), 20, 38 (top), 42, 45, 48, 60 (top), 84 (top), 86 (left), 93, 100, 112, 126 (top), 130 (top), 161, 178 (top)
David Schuppert 30-31, 60 (bottom), 61, 70, 106, 116, 181-82

The following artists are represented by Wilkinson Studios, LLC:
Linda Howard Bittner 33, 72, 90, 195
Bob Brugger 21, 66, 121
Chi Chung 12, 111, 153
Reggie Holladay 23, 74, 75
Gary Krejca 49, 102, 157
Wendy Rasmussen 53, 88, 97
Drew Rose 77, 107, 144
Tammy Smith 38 (bottom), 155
Rich Stergulz 16, 18, 128-29
Kate Sweeney 10-11, 22, 137, 141, 142, 146-47, 191
Carlotta Tormey 4, 5, 78

Photo Credits

The following agencies and individuals have furnished materials to meet the photographic needs of this textbook. We wish to express our gratitude to them for their important contribution.

American Museum of Natural History
Art I Need, Inc.
David Boyd, Jr.
Steve Christopher
George Collins
Corbis
Dr. Stewart Custer
Terry Davenport
Digital Vision
Georgia Department of Natural Resources

Steven Holt
Breck Kent
Joyce Landis
NASA
National Park Service/Elizabeth Joy
PhotoDisc, Inc.
Todd Schneider
Unusual Films
Ward's Natural Science Establishment, Inc.

Cover
PhotoDisc, Inc. (both)
Front Matter
Unusual Films iii; George Collins iv (cells); NASA iv-v (moon); PhotoDisc, Inc. iv-v (all others); Courtesy of the American Museum of Natural History iv-v (skeleton)

Chapter 1
Unusual Films 3, 6 (both), 7, 8; PhotoDisc, Inc. 13, 14 (all)

Chapter 2
Breck Kent 18 (inset); Digital Vision 19; Corbis 20; PhotoDisc, Inc. 23, 24, 26

Chapter 3
PhotoDisc, Inc. 28-29 (all), 30 (top), 34 (both), 35 (all), 36-37 (all others); American Museum of Natural History 31 (bottom); Breck Kent 32; Corbis 37 (bear)

Chapter 4
PhotoDisc, Inc. 40, 41, 50, 54; Unusual Films 42 (both), 45, 46, 48 (both); Dr. Stewart Custer 43 (middle right); Courtesy of Ward's Natural Science Establishment 43 (all others); Steve Christopher 52

Chapter 5
Breck Kent 56 (top left, bottom left), 57 (foreground bottom), 59 (bottom left, top left), 62 (right), 63 (bottom), 65 (top), 67, 69 (top); PhotoDisc, Inc. 56 (top right, bottom right), 57 (right, background), 58 (all), 62 (left, middle), 64 (top middle, bottom), 65 (inset), 66, 68 (top left, bottom left), 69 (middle right), 71 (both); Joyce Landis 59 (right); Dr. Tom Coss 59 (oval inset); ©2002 Art I Need, Inc. 63 (top right); Digital Vision 64 (top left), 68 (top right); Corbis 68-69 (bottom)

Chapter 6
Unusual Films 76 (middle); PhotoDisc, Inc. 76 (all others), 79, 80, 83

Chapter 7
Breck Kent 89 (bottom), 91 (both), 92 (all), 102 (both); PhotoDisc, Inc. 89 (all others), 94 (left, bottom right), 96 (all), 98 (all), 100, 101 (both); Unusual Films 93 (both); Digital Vision 94 (top right); 2002 © Steve Holt/stockpix.com 95; Terry Davenport 99

Chapter 8
PhotoDisc, Inc. 104 (all), 105 (all), 108, 110 (background), 113, 117, 118 (bottom left, bottom right); National Park Service/Elizabeth Joy 109; Unusual Films 110 (bottom), 112; Todd Schneider, Georgia DNR, Wildlife Resources Division 115; Corbis 118 (top left)

Chapter 9
Corbis 122-23 (all others), 124; PhotoDisc, Inc. 123 (far right), 132 (all), 133 (all); Unusual Films 134

Chapter 10
Unusual Films 136 (both), 138 (both), 139, 140, 143 (both), 145 (all), 149, 150; Corbis 148 (both)

Chapter 11
PhotoDisc, Inc. 152, 160 (all); Breck Kent 154 (both); George Collins 156 (both), 157 (background); David W. Boyd, Jr. 157 (inset); Unusual Films 161; Corbis 162

Chapter 12
NASA 165, 166-67 (all), 168, 169, 170 (both), 171, 172-73 (all others), 174-75 (all), 176 (all), 177 (both), 180, 184-85 (all); PhotoDisc, Inc. 172-73 (background), 182-83 (bottom)

Back Matter
Breck Kent 189, 192; PhotoDisc, Inc. 193; David Boyd, Jr. 194; Unusual Films 200 (left)